My Clock Won't Run

By D. Rod Lloyd 2017

Step by Step

No Prior Experience Required

Fourth Edition

Introduction

There are many fine books written for the horologist, apprentice or professional clock shop, but this book is written specifically for a novice clock owner who has an interest in maintaining their own clock as a hobby and does not own a shop full of expensive and complex tools.

Since I started writing, this book has taken on a life of its own. As I proceed through this writing journey, I discovered that most of the clock repair skills can be broken down into simple steps that the average clock owner can understand and follow.

You probably know of or have heard about average people who have started out with a hobby and become just as proficient at their passion as the trained professional, fueled by passion rather than creating a career.

This book assumes the reader has no prior knowledge of the subject and no specialized tools and equipment. Our journey requires a minimal initial outlay.

As a member of NAWCC chapter 31 [National Association of Watch and Clock Collectors], I was persuaded to take over as an instructor of a local hands on clock class. It turns out by teaching this class, I have learned a lot from my students. I discovered clock hobbyists are an incredible sharing group. Each member coming from different backgrounds and experience, each willing to provide suggestions and tips, more of a round table pooling of information.

I own many many clock books and find myself searching through several to find the answers to even the most basic student tasks. This book attempts to put all the basic information you need in one place.

I decided to turn this book into a class workbook, aimed at the new students that walk in at the start of each term with no prior experience, but a loving clock project in their arms. With each project, new questions arise. I decided to document each question/problem and their solutions in this book so all may learn from them. That is why there are so many editions and updates to this work-in-process.

The skills I have learned on my clock journey have turned out to be useful in a surprising number of times and places in my life outside of clocks.

About the Author

My grandfather died when I was seven. We lived in Southport England. He had owned three grandfather clocks. About a year after he died, I asked my mother what happened to the grandfather clocks. She said they were distributed to the grandchildren. I said, "where is mine?" She said I think auntie Florrie got one.

Next time we were visiting auntie Florrie, I said to her "you got my grandfather clock" in a way only an 8-year-old could without being disrespectful. I caught her off guard, but she replied, I could have it when the time was right.

As a kid, whenever I saw an old clock at a jumble sale or going cheap, I would buy it and take it apart to see how it worked. I don't think I ever got one back together again but I enjoyed tinkering with them.

Twenty years later when I was getting married, now living in the USA, auntie Florrie wrote to me saying I could now have the clock.

I arranged to have the clock shipped over and it was proudly placed in the entrance hall to my home. It was built in about 1880 in Maghull England by a local clockmaker, had

a stately mahogany case, hand painted dial and ran nicely.

After a few years, it stopped. I was frustrated that I didn't know what was wrong with it or how to get it going. I ended up having it serviced by a local repair shop and it ran again. I was fascinated with the clock.

In 1995, my family decided to spend a year in England including putting the kids in school. It was a big challenge to arrange to swap houses with an English family. Finally, we were settled and the kids started school, my wife was volunteering at a local charity shop and suddenly I had time on my hands.

I read the paper that morning and came across an ad for a clock course starting nearby at Manchester City College. I called the college and they told me it was a three-year course, one day per week. I explained I was only in the country for one year, so I persuaded them to let me take the course, coming all three days.

I enjoyed the course and did very well. The final exam took several weeks, making a 'suspension bridge' from scratch to exact specifications, restoring several old clocks and watches. I documented the process and took the extensive final written exam all set by BHI [British Horological Institute]. I did pass the exams and became a Horologist.

20 years later I teach clock repair classes and 'pass it on'. This is the class workbook.

Table of Contents

...................**Error! Bookmark not defined.**

Introduction.....................3

About the Author.....................5

Table of Contents 7

What is a Clock? 9

What is Time? 9

Introduction.....................10

First things First 11

Wall Clock Beat 12

Mantel or Shelf Clock.....................12

Setting the Beat of the Pendulum Clock 13

Leveling.....................15

If it Still Stops 15

Oiling the Clock 16

Very Dirty Movement 19

Removing the Hands 20

Time Regulation.....................22

Replacing a Lost Key 23

Taking Clock Care to the Next Level.............24

Clock 'Fun'damentals.....................24

Escapement 28

    Anchor Escapement 28

    Deadbeat Escapement 29

Diagnosis 32

Beginners Clock Repair Tool Kit for $85........35

Magnification.....................40

Taking the Movement Apart.....................44

The Diagram 46

Cleaning the Parts.....................51

Pegging 54

Making Repairs 55

    Pivot Polishing 56

Straightening Bent Pivots & Arbors........63

Replacing a Broken or Worn Out Pivot...64

Bushing Using Hand Tools.....................67

Using the Bushing Machine.....................72

Repairing a Broken Tooth 77

    Lantern Pinion Repair.....................80

    Repairing Bent Escape Wheel Teeth.......81

Motion Work 83

ClickWork 84

Mainsprings 85

Reassembly 88

Striking Setup 90

Lubricating the Movement 98

Test Run 99

Going Electronic.....................100

Refinishing the Clock Case 101

Anniversary Clocks.....................103

Cuckoo Clocks.....................104

Length of a Pendulum 108

If the Suspension spring is missing.............109

Watches 110

The Lathe 113

Clock Marts 116

Lessons Learned 117

Conclusion.....................119

Clock and Watch Associations 120

Clock Supply Houses 120

Horological Tools 121

Horological Book Sellers 121

Frequently Asked Student Questions 122

Cuckoo Clock Questions 127

What is a Clock?

This might sound like a dumb question. Isn't it obvious?

If my family heirloom clock were to stop working and I was to take out the mechanical movement and install an inexpensive battery quartz movement, is it still my favorite clock? It probably would keep better time. It wouldn't need weekly winding. I might not be able to see any difference on the outside, but I would know. Chances are I would not be happy with the upgrade. So, is the clock the movement?

What if the clock fell off the wall and the case was badly damaged. I decide to install the old movement into a new case. Is it still my clock? Heck no.

What if the movement and case were fine but I replaced the dial and hands. Is it still my clock? It would be like one of the family members had full-on plastic surgery.

What if I replace the deep striking gong to a small bell. Is it still my clock? It would be like a family member changed from a man's voice to a ladies voice [or something similar].

So, it appears a clock is the sum of the case, the dial and hands, the sounds and the movement.

What is Time?

Many have struggled to come up with a good definition for 'Time'.

At a local college science competition, I adjudicate a subject about time, and I ask the advanced students to define time. I get a lot of strange answers.

What is your definition?

Look at the last page in this book for my suggested definition.

Introduction

Mechanical clocks are now considered works of art, a part of history, a member of the family, and they need *love*.

Sooner or later, your treasured timepiece will stop. Your choice is to either live with it in silence or go to a hard to find clock repair shop, leave it for weeks and pay perhaps hundreds of dollars to get it back, hopefully working.

The fact is, you can more than likely do the same thing they do, yourself. There are little-known items that stop a clock that you can easily do yourself for very little money. You can even oil your clock for just a few dollars' worth of oil.

You can service Grandfather Clocks, Mantel Clocks, Wall Clocks, Kitchen Clocks, French Clocks, Cuckoo Clocks, etc. No expensive tools needed besides oil which I will tell you where to buy it very inexpensively.

I will teach you how to service your own clock. If your child or pet were to get sick, you would get medical help and pay whatever it took to make them better. Why not treat your treasured clock the same way.

This book is a general overview of mechanical pendulum clocks and does not refer to any particular clock style or make.

There are endless case styles and clock makers; each has its own design, personality, and moods. I have kept the information somewhat generic and the procedures very inexpensive. This is just a start of a new journey. There are almost as many clock books as there are clocks. They tend to spend too much time on theory and the unnecessarily complicated stuff. I have purposefully kept this basic so I don't lose you but feel free to go on and explore other fine books written on clock repair as you get comfortable. Look at YouTube and you will find many videos with lots of helpful information. I write this as a horologist, not an English major.

I will start very slowly with the basics. Bear with me.

First things First

If your clock has stopped, the first thing to check [forgive the obvious] is if it is wound up. If it needs winding, go ahead and wind it up now. It will only wind up one way. If clockwise doesn't work, try counter clockwise. It usually takes about twelve to sixteen full turns to wind a clock but your clock might be a little different. You should hear a clicking of the ratchet as you wind. If it does not turn either way, don't force it, it is likely fully wound.

Contrary to popular belief, you cannot overwind a clock [or watch]. If it is fully wound and does not run, something else is wrong. If you have lost the key or winding crank, see the chapter later on for ordering a new key.

If you wind the clock but it never gets fully wound, perhaps it makes a shuddering sound, the mainspring is broken. We will deal with that later.

There might be more than one winding hole. Be sure to wind up all of them.

If your clock has weights, you might need to pull the chains to wind up the clock [like cuckoo clocks etc]. Pull the loose chain that does not have the weight attached. Hold the clock as you pull the chain so you don't pull it off the wall. If the chain will not pull, it is likely off the sprocket and needs servicing.

Now the clock is wound up, give the pendulum a little push and listen to what the clock tells you. Listen for its ticking. It will most likely start ticking but might slow down and stop.

If it has an uneven tick - tock, you need to adjust its "beat". It is most likely a little out of level. It takes a lot more power for a clock to run when it's out of beat, extra power your clock can't supply, especially if it has not been serviced recently.

Set the hands to the correct time by turning the minute hand only, turning it forwards only. Some clocks can be damaged by turning them backward.

Wall Clock Beat

If the tick and the toc are not even, your clock is out of beat. Move the bottom of the clock a little to the left, say ¼". If the tick - tock is worse, try moving the bottom ¼" to the other side. Experiment by moving it left and right until the tick - tock is even.

Mantel or Shelf Clock

Again listen to the tick - tock on the clock and see if it is nice, even tick-tock. It should sound steady and even like a metronome. There should be equal time between the TICK and the TOCK. The pendulum needs to swing exactly equal distances from the dead center to the left, as from dead center to the right. If a clock is out of beat, the pendulum will swing for a few minutes, then stop even if the clock case is level.

Setting the Beat of the Pendulum Clock

If the beat is irregular like tock,tick------ tock,tick- an adjustment must be made or the clock will stop. This can be done by either leveling again from left to right or by moving the clock very slightly from the bottom until you hear the most even tick-tock. This may not be physically level for the clock case.

If this fails or you don't wish to have a clock case crooked on your wall or shelf, you may take off the pendulum and *slightly* move the pendulum leader from left to right or right to left until it almost or starts moving back and forth on its own. This will only work if the leader is a friction fit between the pallet arbor and the crutch.

1. Move the pendulum slowly to the right until a tic is heard.
2. Release the pendulum.
3. If there is another tic, go to 5.
4. If there is not another tic, move fork or peg to the right and return to 1.
5. Move the pendulum to the left, until a tic is heard.
6. Release the pendulum.
7. If there is another tick, the clock is in beat.
8. If there is not another beat, move the fork or peg to the left and return to 1.

If it does not have a friction fit, you will need to bend the crutch wire. It should have the same feel from dead center to right and dead center to left. Re-hang the pendulum and the clock should run and you are done.

If winding and setting the beat has not solved the problem, continue on.

Hands have to be free! Make sure the hands are free from touching each other. Also, make sure the hands are not touching the dial [or glass] at any point. If the hands are touching, this will stop the clock. Slightly

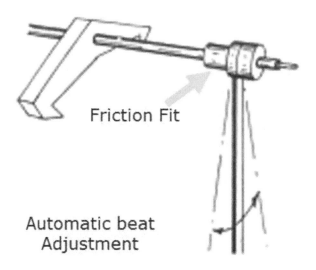

Friction Fit

Automatic beat Adjustment

bend the hands away from each other by holding the hand still toward the center and slightly pulling the hands away from each other.

Is the Pendulum dragging? Look into the lower side window and watch the pendulum swing. If the pendulum is touching the chime rods toward the back or touching the weights toward the front, the pendulum will stop. This indicates a problem in leveling from front to rear. Read later.

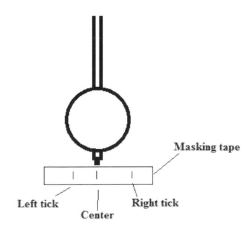

Masking tape

Left tick   Right tick
Center

Place some masking tape just below the pendulum rating nut and mark its position 'at rest'. Move the pendulum slowly to the right until you hear a tick and accurately mark the position. Then move the pendulum slowly to the left until you hear a tick and carefully mark the position. If the distances from the center are not equal, as in my diagram, the crutch/fork needs adjusting.

Some clocks have a beat scale at the bottom of the pendulum which makes this process much easier.

Leveling

Your clock will need to be level from front to back and side to side.

Place a small temporary shim or coin [about 1/8th of an inch or less] under one side of the clock. If the tick tock is worse try the shim under the other side. Experiment with different thicknesses of shims until the tick and tock are even.

shim

If it Still Stops

If the clock still stops when the tick and tock are even, there is one more basic task to try. Open the front and any rear door. Advance the minute hand to about five past the hour, pausing to allow any striking or chiming to complete, then remove both hands. Take off the pendulum and put it back on carefully. Remove the dial and try the clock again. It is possible one of these items is binding. If it runs with these removed, put them back, one at a time until the problem returns and you have likely found the problem. Study this area, track down the problem, correct and retest.

If still no luck, we will need to go to the next level. Most likely the clock will need oiling. The fact that the clock stopped is a good thing, it is trying to tell you something. If it continued to run with no oil, it would cause a lot of wear and damage the clock seriously. Consider the clock stopping as

"The oil light is on".

Correcting Beat

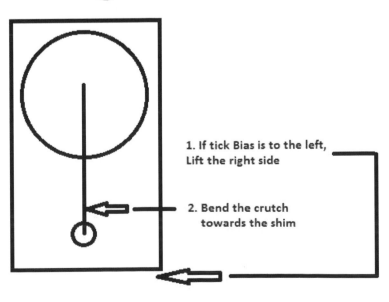

1. If tick Bias is to the left, Lift the right side

2. Bend the crutch towards the shim

Oiling the Clock

We can try to oil the clock first of all without removing the clock from its case. You have a 50% chance this will correct the problem.

The most important thing to remember is to ensure that you only use clock oil. Using substitutes like WD40 can actually damage your movement.

Just like regular oil changes extend the life of your car's engine, regular clock oiling extends the life of your clock. Oiling your clock every five years will prevent expensive clock repairs and ensure that your clock will last for the generations to come. Imagine never changing your car's oil; it wouldn't take long for the engine to seize. Without regular oiling, your clock will end up requiring a major service, or possibly a new movement.

If your clock has a rear door, open the door to expose the rear of the clock. Remove the pendulum from its hook. Never move a clock with its pendulum attached or it will likely damage the movement.

You will notice multiple oil sinks on the surface of the clock plate. Oil sinks are located where the ends of the steel arbor meet the clock plate. Please refer to the picture and diagram showing an oil sink.

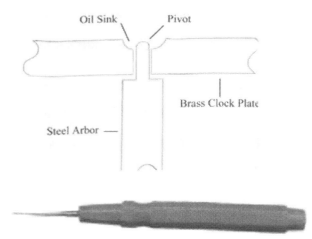

and the screws holding the clock dial on. When the clock movement is exposed, follow the instructions above.

To oil a clock, apply ONE drop of oil to each oil sink. Use a magnifying glass to see better. Don't try and fill the oil sink, because the oil is held in place by capillary attraction and surface tension. If you apply too much oil, the surface tension will not hold and the oil will run down the plate, leaving the bearing dry. Repeat the oiling process for all visible oil sinks. Oil the front of the clock with extreme care. Do not oil the wheel/pinion teeth during this process; they need to stay dry to maintain an efficient working condition.

If your clock has a front door, open it. You might need to remove the hands [see blow]

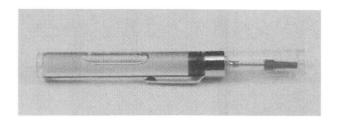

A better oiler is this Precision Dip Oiler below. It has a spade-like tip to hold a small amount of oil.

The eye of a very small sewing needle will usually carry the right amount of oil. Just wet the pivot.

It is best if you actually take the movement out of the case altogether if you can. It is most likely screwed to the case with four screws. With the movement completely out of the case, you can blow out all the dust and debris with a can of compressed air and then oil the movement completely, front and back plates as stated above.

When it is all oiled up, put the movement back in the case [not including the clock dial and hands yet] and attach the pendulum. Test the clock like before making sure it is in beat with an even tick - tock. It should run now. Let it run for a full day and then put the dial back on and re-install the hands.

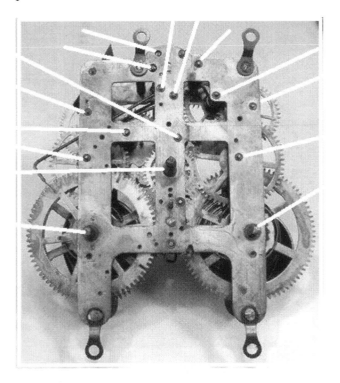

Do not be tempted to take the movement apart at this point. Even if the spring does not appear to be wound up, it is still likely under some power and the spring can open violently causing damage to the movement and injury to you. If you do want to take the movement apart, please read this entire book first.

Very Dirty Movement

It is possible to clean the old oil and dirt off a movement without dismantling it. It is much preferred it be dismantled, but if you do not want to go to that level, obtain a water-based clock cleaning solution from

www.merritts.com, or

www.ronellclock.com or

www.timesavers.com

Place some clock cleaning solution on a soft cloth. Do not make the cloth too wet. The movement should not be flooded with cleaning solution. You can make a clock cleaning solution by mixing eight parts ammonia to one part commercial liquid cleanser, and one part oil soap. Use the soft cloth to rub off grease and grime that's stuck to easy-to-reach parts of the movement. Do not force the cloth into tight areas, as small parts might break.

Dab some clock cleaning solution on a cotton swab or Q-tip. Insert into difficult-to-reach parts inside the clock movement. Rub gently to remove grease and grime.

Check the movement's wheels to see if they move freely, by gently manipulating the various parts with your fingers. Place a small amount of clock oil on a soft cloth. Clock oil is a special product available from retailers. Do not use WD-40 as it may clog the movement. Lubricate only those parts that already have oil. Not all parts of the movement need to be lubricated, but those that do, vary from movement to movement. Use the soft cloth to lubricate parts that are

easily reached. Put some clock oil on a cotton swab to lubricate smaller, or hidden parts inside the movement.

Alternatively, soak the whole movement for about 20 minutes in the solution. After it has soaked, run lots of hot water over the movement to rinse off the cleaning solution and then dry the movement thoroughly using a hair dryer or in your kitchen oven. It is very important you get every drop of water dried off. Then proceed to oil the clock.

Removing the Hands

Pin & Collet

Look closely at the arbor of your clock on which the minute and hour hands are mounted. Use a magnifying glass to see if a metal pin is passing through the arbor, parallel to the clock dial. If you see one, your clock hands are held by a pin and collet.

Take a pair of needle nose pliers and pull out the pin. The pin should be tapered, so pull from the fatter end.

Lift off the minute hand, then the collet. Next, lift off the hour hand. On some clocks, the hour hand will have a small clip or screw holding it in place, which you will need to simply remove.

Threaded Hand Nut

Look for a metal nut with a serrated edge screwed onto the minute hand. If you find one, your clock's hands are held with a threaded hand nut.

Undo the hand nut by holding the minute hand as closely to the nut as possible to prevent it from accidentally bending.

Unscrew the hand nut with your free hand and lift off the minute hand, followed by the hour hand. Note that some clocks have a slotted nut instead of a hand nut, which requires a special tool.

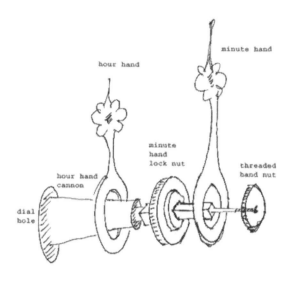

Friction Fit

Look at the arbor of the clock for a pin or hand nut. If neither are present, the clock hands are being held on by friction alone.

Grip the minute hand at the arbor and carefully pull it off.

Grip the hour hand and pull it off. Never try to pry friction fit clock hands off with a screwdriver as they may get damaged or the dial of the clock could get scratched.

Adjusting the Crutch

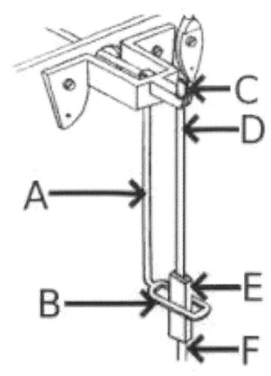

A: Crutch Arm
B: Crutch Fork
C: Top Suspension Block
D: Suspension Spring
E: Lower Suspension Block
F: Pendulum Rod

Once you have the clock running and the tick – tock even, you will want to adjust the crutch so it will run correctly without the shims.

Identify the Crutch Arm on your clock using the diagram above. Using a pair of needle-nose pliers, bend the wire a very small amount in the direction you have the shims. Remove the shims and listen for an even tick – tock. Continue bending the crutch arm until the tick – tock is even without the shims.

Time Regulation

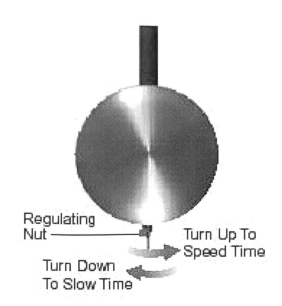

Regulating Nut ——— Turn Up To Speed Time

Turn Down To Slow Time

Regulation or the act of adjusting the rate or speed of a clock is a simple series of repeated steps until the desired effect is achieved. This is accomplished by governing the location of the center of gravity along the length of the pendulum.

While many factors may affect the timekeeping rate of your clock, none will as much as changes in the ambient temperature of its environment, assuming the mechanics are in good working order as excessive friction from any source can have an adverse effect on the timekeeping ability of the movement. Every moving part must be in good condition and properly lubricated so the gear train can operate as freely as possible. Friction leads to wear which is your clocks enemy number one.

Once you have observed a change in timekeeping over the course of several days it is time to begin the regulation procedure. Keep a pad and pen handy for recording notes; include the starting error and all

adjustments you make as this will greatly assist the process. Remember to use a rate of error that is consistent such as minutes or seconds per 24 hours, and to use the same time source for making all of your comparisons.

Adjusting the pendulum shorter will cause your clock to run faster while lengthening it causes it to run slower or simply put "speedup, slowdown".

Look for the rating nut at the base of the pendulum which is what raised or lowers the pendulum disk or bob. Remember that the pendulum disk may become wedged against the rod, especially in the case of a wooden stick and some help may be needed. Turning the rating nut without affecting the disk has no bearing on timekeeping.

By turning the rating nut to the right the disk will raise, which will make the clock faster while turning it left will lower the disk and make the clock slower. The rule of thumb is one turn of the regulating nut equals one minute per 24 hours, but your results may prove different and that is what makes the note keeping important to your success. By recording your actions 3 or 4 daily sessions is normally all that is needed. You should not try or expect to correct the error in one session, but rather try to split the difference by half each session, slowly sneaking up on the error without overshooting or see-sawing back and forth.

It will not be possible to make the movement timekeeping perfectly accurate.

Replacing a Lost Key

Measure the size of the winding arbor carefully and using the chart, order a replacement key from www.ronellclock.com, www.timesavers.com or www.Merritts.com

Clock key sizing chart

Shaft width / Key

- 1.75mm = 000 Key
- 2.0mm = 00 Key
- 2.25mm = 0 Key
- 2.5mm = 1 Key
- 2.75mm = 2 Key
- 3.0mm = 3 Key
- 3.25mm = **4 Key**
- 3.5mm = 5 Key
- 3.75mm = 6 Key

Shaft width / Key

- 4.0mm = 7 Key
- 4.25mm = **8 Key**
- 4.5mm = 9 Key
- 4.75mm = 10 Key
- 5.00mm = 11 Key
- 5.25mm = 12 Key
- 5.5mm = 13 Key
- 5.75mm = 14 Key
- 6.0mm = 15 Key

Be careful if you are measuring the exposed end of the winding arbor. Many are tapered and the new key will not slide on far enough to be safe.

If you plan on repairing clocks, it is a good idea to own a set of bench keys. In that case, test the size that fits your clock, and order a replacement key based on the size selected.

If you own a set of let-down keys, use this as your guide

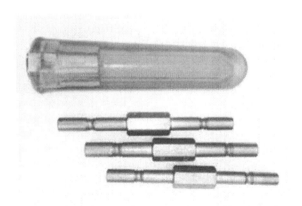

Taking Clock Care to the Next Level

If the above information does not get your clock running and you want to do some actual maintenance to your clock, strip it down for a full cleaning, repair wear, do not despair there is plenty more you can do. I will walk you through it.

Clock 'Fun'damentals

A crude clock needs three basic items.

1. Power – spring or weights.
2. Means of regulating the power to a calculated period – an escapement.
3. Means of viewing the results – clock dial and hands.

When you look at a clock movement, you will see a bunch of gears. We call them wheels in the clock world. What do they all do?

In a very simple clock, we have three wheels.

The great wheel contains the mainspring or is driven by the weights which supply the power to the intermediate wheel which runs the hour hand and drives the escape wheel. The escape wheel has a time regulator called an escapement and pendulum. A typical three wheel train will run for about a day [actually 30 hours]. The large wheel of the great wheel [the leader] drives the [follower] small wheel [pinion] on the next wheel [intermediate wheel] in the train and so on until you get to the escapement. We call the wheels T1, T2 and T3. [T stands for Time]

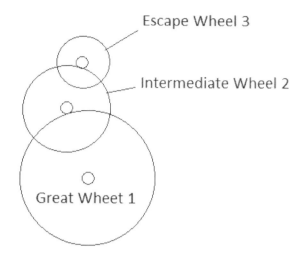

Three Wheel Train

Sidebar A pinion can be cut from solid metal [leaf style] or made up of steel rods [trundles or pins] in between brass ends caps or shrouds [lantern pinion].

If we add a fourth wheel it will typically run for a week because of the gearing. In this case, we have T1, T2, T3 and T4.

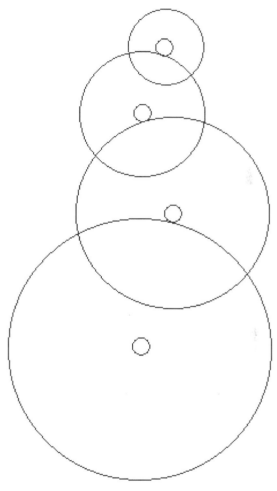

Four Wheel Train

and if we add a fifth wheel it will typically run for a month because of the gearing, in which case we have T1, T2, T3, T4 and T5.

This is assuming the clock is a 'time only' [no striking or chiming]. This rule of 3 wheels, 4 wheels, and 5 wheels is only used as an example. There are many contradictions to this rule depending on the teeth ratios.

To add striking we must add a second 'train' to drive that function.

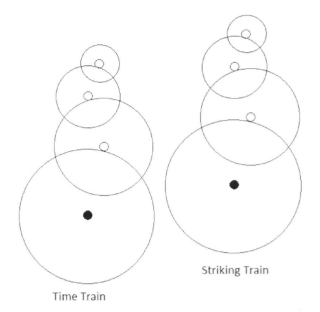

Time Train   Striking Train

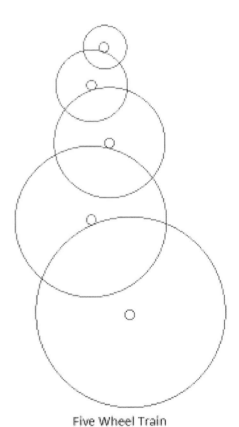

Five Wheel Train

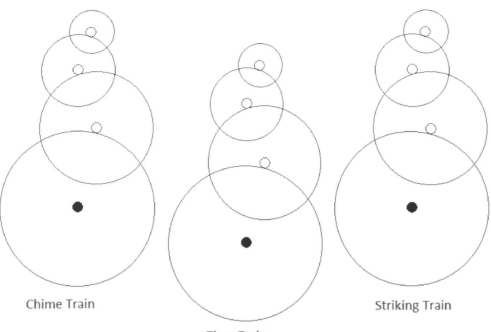

Chime Train

Time Train

Striking Train

And if we add chiming also, we have a three train movement which looks pretty complicated. But note, each train acts independently with only a lever that trips the next train.

Note the three winding holes on the clock below and how they match up with the arbors on the three great wheels in the above diagram.

Escapement

I will keep the description of the escapement very basic.

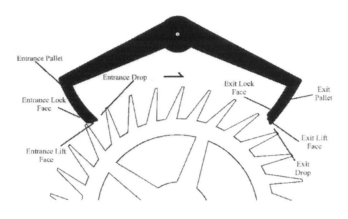

The job of the escapement is to regulate the time. Without it, the wheels would run wildly fast until the spring wound down or the weights hit the floor. The escapement will only allow the escape wheel to advance one tooth at a time with each swing of the pendulum. The design of the pendulum determines how fast each tooth advances. Using calculations of the gearing and the length of the pendulum, the clock is designed to it keep time.

The most common types of escapement you will encounter are:

Invented around 1657, the anchor quickly superseded the older and inaccurate verge to become the standard escapement used in pendulum clocks through the 19th century. The anchor is responsible for the long narrow shape of most pendulum clocks, and for the development of the longcase or tall case clock [grandfather clock].

The anchor consists of an escape wheel with pointed, backward slanted teeth, and an "anchor"-shaped piece pivoted above it which rocks from side to side, linked to the pendulum. The anchor has slanted pallets on the arms which alternately catch on the teeth of the escape wheel, receiving impulses.

Deadbeat escapement showing:
(a) Escape wheel
(b) Pallets
(c) Pendulum crutch.

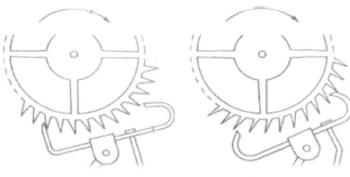

Recoil   Dead-beat

Graham Dead-Beat Escapement

Recoil Escapement

Note the teeth are pointing in different directions.

The Graham or deadbeat escapement was an improvement of the anchor. In the anchor escapement, the swing of the pendulum pushes the escape wheel backward during part of its cycle. This 'recoil' disturbs the motion of the pendulum, causing inaccuracy, and reverses the direction of the gear train, causing a backlash and introducing high loads into the system, leading to friction and wear. The main advantage of the deadbeat is that it eliminated recoil. The teeth point forwards.

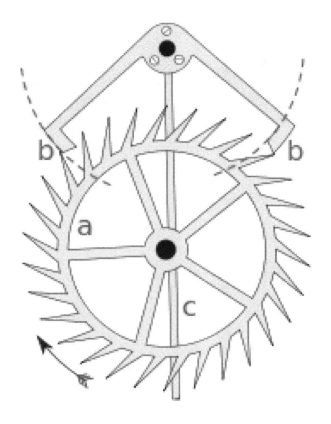

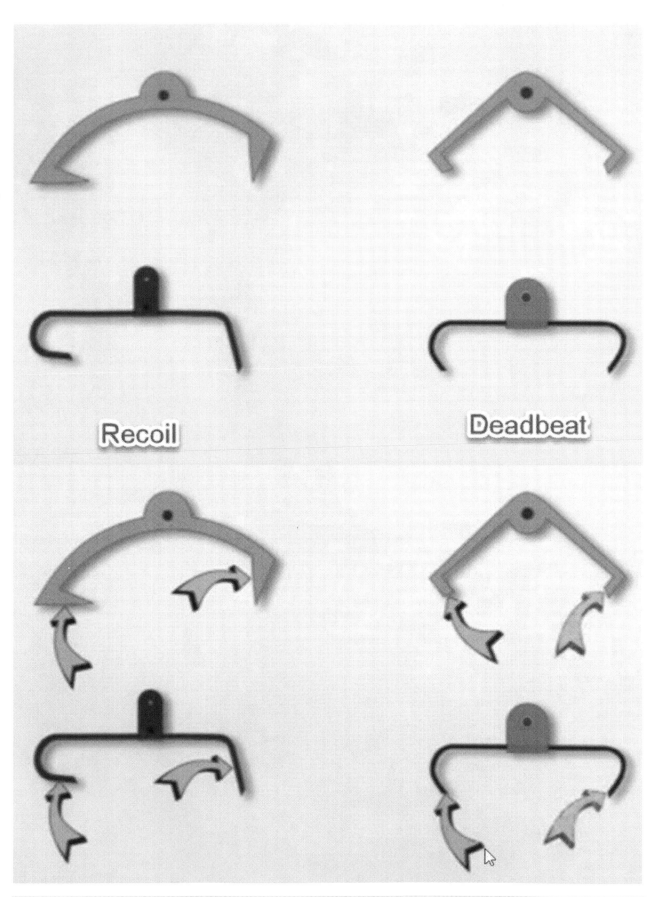

Recoil

Deadbeat

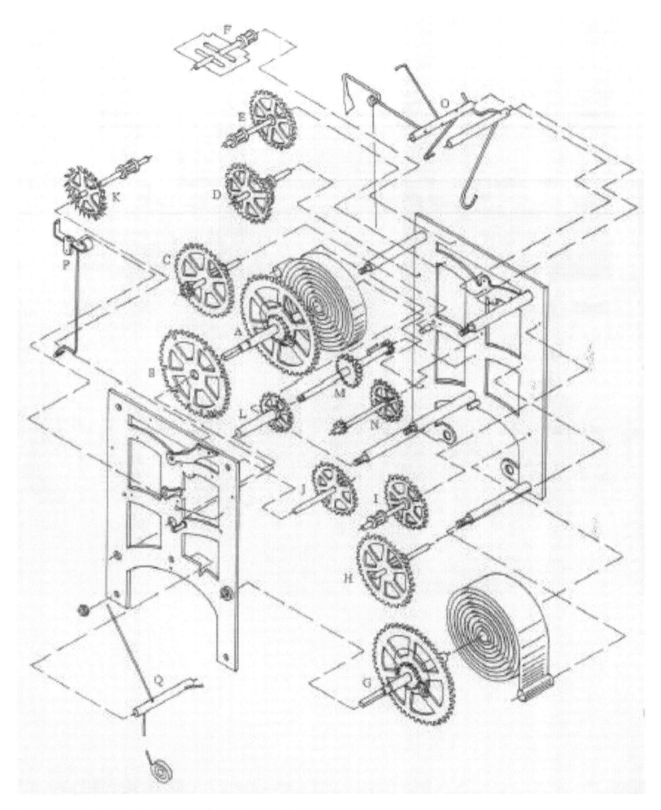

Because this book is directed to the novice
owner, I will leave chiming to future editions.

Diagnosis

If your clock has stopped, you are sure it is fully wound up and it is in-beat, there are two basic reasons it would stop.

1. Escapement Problem
2. Loss of Power

Escapement Problem

Look very closely at the escapement. If a pallet is 'hung up' on the tip of an escape wheel tooth, mark the tooth with a marking pen and restart the clock. If the same tooth is involved repeatedly, the likelihood is that tooth is bent, or the tooth that has just left the opposite pallet is bent. To check and correct the fault see next section.

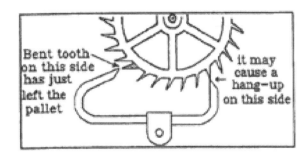

Loss of Power

If neither pallet is touching a tooth when you test its operation, that is, if the pallets are hanging freely between the escape wheel teeth, and if the pallets can be rocked without either one touching a tooth, and it is properly adjusted as above, then the clock has stopped because there is little or no power being transmitted to the escapement.

The Enemy

A clock is designed with approximately 10% additional power than is needed to run in perfect condition. This is to allow for a small amount of wear, and oils in less than perfect condition.

The enemy of a clock is friction. Clock oil gets 'gummy' because it tends to absorb the dust in the air. This gum will cause additional friction and stop the clock. The only way to remove the old gummy oil is to take the movement apart. I will explain this later.

A second problem which is worse. The oil may have evaporated or run out, leaving the pivots to run dry, metal grinding on metal. The pivot connected to the wheel arbor is usually made of steel. The front and back movement plates that support the wheel/pivot are usually made of brass. You will note that brass is a softer metal than steel so the movement plate tends to wear the most. This is by design so the plates will wear and protect the pivot. The plates are easier to repair than replacing pivots.

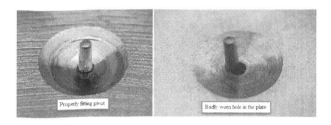

Properly fitting pivot | Badly worn hole in the plate

The pivot may also have some wear.

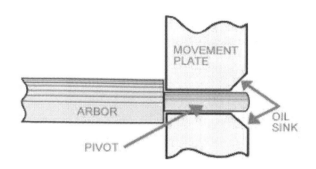

MOVEMENT PLATE

ARBOR

OIL SINK

PIVOT

Imagine rubbing two pieces of sandpaper across each other. It will be hard due to the friction of the rough surfaces.

Now, imagine sliding two wet pieces of glass past each other. They will glide easily. That is the effect we are looking for. See later for the procedure to create this.

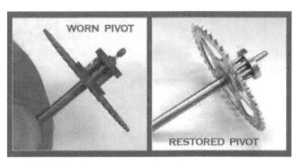

WORN PIVOT

RESTORED PIVOT

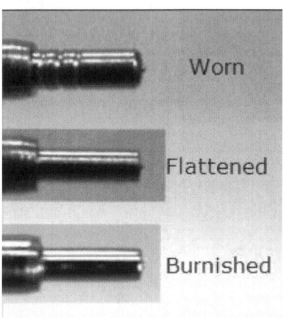

Worn

Flattened

Burnished

Escapement Pallet Wear

It is also important to polish the impulse faces of the escapement. I have found, if you only do one thing to a clock, polishing the pallet faces will have the most improvement. Make sure you don't change any angles of the pallet faces.

The wear must be ground out and then polished. This is accomplished with a series of emery boards of different grits in a way that removes the least amount of metal and maintains the original angles. If too much metal is removed or the angles are changed, the pallets must be reshaped or bent in order for them to be adjusted properly once they are put back in the clock movement.

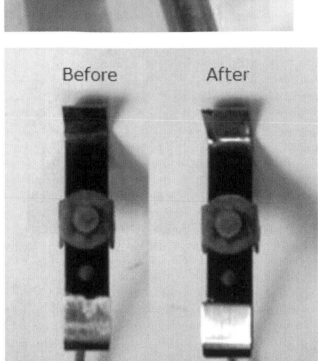

Before   After

Beginners Clock Repair Tool Kit for $85

[2017]

Getting started in clock repair can be intimidating, especially when you consider the tools that many clock repair people have.

I have created a list of tools that a beginner can get by with and do a lot of the work we do.

The fact is, 90% of what we do is performed with 10% of our tools. The basic idea is this list is well thought out, inexpensive and will get someone started without breaking the bank or putting you off getting started.

The First Set of tools most people will already have [or should have] around the house:

Needle nose pliers
Small square nose pliers with wire cutters
Screwdrivers slotted medium 1/4" tip
Screwdrivers slotted small 1/8" tip
Wet & dry sandpaper 500, 1000, 1500 & 2500 grit [available from auto parts store]
Cordless drill or Dremel [to act as a lathe]
Popsicle sticks or tongue depressors
Toothpicks
Tweezers fine and stout
Hammer small
Pocket knife
Empty containers and zip-lock bags for loose parts

The Second Set will likely need to be purchased from a specialty house like:
Merrits www.merritts.com or
Timesavers www.timesavers.com.
Numbers are the Timesavers part number

Cleaning solution concentrate pint *17863*	$11
Clock oil *13839*	$ 2
3 Movement assembly posts *13408*	$15
Set of 2 mainspring clamps *20082*	$ 7
Letdown key set *15808*	$37
Mainspring Winder *13473*	$10
Loupe 2x, 5x *15870 & 18213*	$ 3
TOTAL	**$85**

The Third Set I call a "Bushing Kit" will be needed if you want to repair worn bushings.

Bushings 2 $4 each [Bergeon #7 & #9]	$ 8
Bush reamer [Bergeon #247]	$20
Handle for reamers	$12
Cutting Broach set .031" - .090"	$14
Smoothing Broaches .0314 & .0374	$ 7
TOTAL	**$61**

Note: I suggest Bergeon bushing. K&D are just as good but they are not interchangeable so stick to one or the other.

Get a shoe box or tackle box to keep them organized.

Then we start getting into the more advanced and specialized tools, which can be purchased one at a time as needed.

Cleaning Solution

You can buy a readymade concentrate from the parts house [which is what I recommend] or you can make your own at home using the following recipe:

4 oz. oleic acid [Use Murphy's Oil Soap]

8 oz. Acetone

12 oz. 26% Ammonium Hydroxide

1 Gallon Water

Let soak for 5 minutes then scrub the parts with an old toothbrush.

Do not use laundry or dish detergent as a substitute for oleic acid. Detergent will pit, darken the brass in a variegated form, and will generally ruin the finish on brass clock parts.

Clock Oil

I recommend Mobil 1 – 5W-30
Its formula and viscosity are perfect for clocks.
Sushhhh don't tell them, they will put the price up.

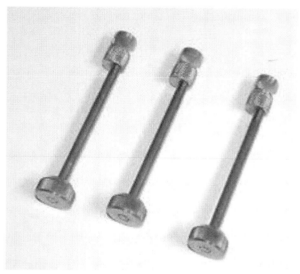

Movement Assembly Posts

You need these so you can disassemble the movement. The movement should be disassembled horizontally. There are usually several items protruding from the plate so it will not sit flat on the table. The posts raise the movement up clear of the protruding items.

You can, of course, cut some holes in a small cardboard box and set the movement on that.

Mainspring Clamps

These are used to contain the mainspring while the movement is disassembled. Without containing the spring, the spring could cause injury to you or damage the clock when disassembling. 1-15/16" diameter is the most common size, or buy the set for a little more.

A fellow NAWCC member uses a toilet roll to support his movement – clock movement that is. 🙂

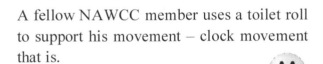

You can also use sturdy wire instead.

Homemade Letdown Key

A satisfactory letdown key can be made from a 6" piece of wood closet pole [1 ¼" dowel] or even an old broom handle. Drill a hole in the end, then a slot to fit your clock key. The clock key will fit in this slot and you can grip the pole to let down the movement.

Check out my homemade lathe using a Dremel. I use it for quick pivot polishing and it is very portable and does not take up much space. Note, I have added the three jaw chuck to my setup.

I am not suggesting you never buy clock tools. The fact is many people enjoy buying old clock tools at marts and specialty tools from the supply houses as much as collecting the clocks they are used on. I own some tools I have never used and some I don't even know what they do!

Magnification

There are times when you need to see better than your normal vision, be it by the naked eye or with normal prescription glasses. If you use reading glasses, of course, you should use them for normal work. When you need extra help, we have several choices.

First, we need to define some terms.

Magnification – how many times bigger the object is seen.

Focal length – The distance from the lens to the object that is in focus. Typically the stronger the magnification, the closer you need to be to your work. Some lenses have longer focal lengths than others and the longer focal length can be easier to work with, especially for longer periods. Also, there are times when looking at an object inside a movement, you will not be able to get close enough to get it in focus if you have a short focal length.

Magnifiation for typical Reading Glasses Diopters	
Diopter	Magnification
1	1.25
1.5	1.375
2	1.5
2.5	1.625
3	1.75
4	2

Field of vision – How large an area is in focus at any given time.

Stronger reading glasses. If you normally use say 1.5 diopter glasses, consider having some stronger bench glasses. Try the strongest you can find. Lope 2 ½ x, 5 x &/or Optivisor 2 ½ x with a focal length of 8"

I actually keep a strong pair of dime store reading glasses on my bench. I normally use 1.5 diopters but for close up work, I find 4.0 or even 5.0 diopter work great and easier to wear than a loupe.

Loupes have long been favored for detail clockwork. They usually don't specify the focal length when for sale. You will likely accumulate a variety that works for various types of work, and favor one you prefer. Ideally, buy at a mart where you can try them out before buying. Loupes can be held in the eye, clipped to glasses or on a wire around the head.

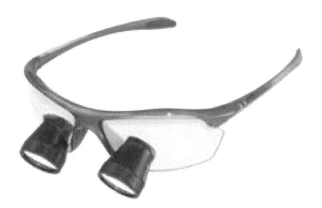

A more recent choice is the Optivisor. They come in various magnifications and often have a longer focal length. They provide magnification to both eyes and this also helps with judging distance, especially working with tools. They are comfortable to wear and can even include a light but the light does make it heavier.

The ultimate in magnification is the microscope. This is most often used at a fixed workstation like over a lathe.

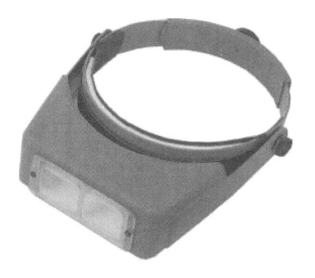

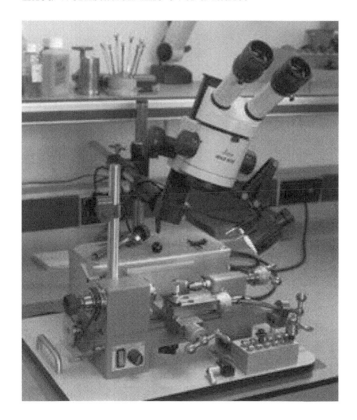

More recently the surgeon's loupe is becoming popular but they can be very expensive. They usually have a longer focal length and good field of vision.

With the invention of the quartz movement, professional, full-time clock, and watch repairers have almost become extinct, leaving a plethora of old and fascinating tools to harvest.

All I suggest is you get your feet wet first. I read a beginner book recently that contained 41 pages on tools. It is enough to put anybody off considering tinkering with clocks. I have amassed many tools over the years, some of which I have made myself and cherish them. My clock shop [more of a nook] is always a fun place to show off to visiting friends and guest who are fascinated.

By joining a local clock club, you will develop friendships and contacts with experienced members that will likely work with you and allow you to use their specialised tools as needed.

Clock Repair Checklist

The first thing we must do is inspect the movement for obvious defects. Use this checklist after you have removed the movement from the case and let down the mainspring.

- Look at the condition of the oil [gummy, dry, over oiling]
- Check the clickwork for wear
- Note any defects in the suspension spring
- Closely observe the action of the escapement with a loupe
- Make sure all the teeth of the escape wheel are correctly shaped
- Note any missing or damaged teeth
- Check for wear in the escapement pallets
- Make sure all wheels have drop [endshake]
- Check the pivot holes for wear
- Observe the mesh of all wheels to pinions
- Observe the condition of the mainspring [if visible]
- Create diagrams and photos of the movement

Dismantle the movement

- Inspect the pivots for wear

Taking the Movement Apart

To clean out the old gummy oil and to repair the worn pivot and pivot hole, we must take the movement apart. No whining, get it done. We need to perform our work using the surgeon's rule "Do No Harm".

When taking off the pendulum, it is best to mark where it sits on the rating screw. Scribe a line across the top of the bob, on the pendulum rod. Assuming it was well regulated before you started work, this will save much time in regulating the clock when you put it back together. Alternatively, place a piece of masking tape around the rating nut so it will not get changed.

If the clock has weights, remove the weights BEFORE you remove the pendulum.

Assuming the movement is already out of its case, we need to identify if the movement is powered by weights or by a spring. This is obvious if it is powered by weights and they will long since have been removed and set aside, but if it is powered by a spring, it is extremely important that the power is 'let down'. If the movement were to be opened up while the spring is wound up, even just a small amount, the movement would explode so to speak as soon and the teeth start to disengage, letting the wheels run wild which could cause injury to the repairer and cause severe damage to the movement at the same time. How we do this will depend on the type of movement.

This wheel came from a clock that was opened up without letting down the mainspring fully. It has:

- Dislodged the wheel from its arbor
- Twisted the wheel
- Bent the wheel out of round
- Bent two teeth beyond straightening

If the spring is contained within a barrel [typically in European clocks], it can be let down completely and it is safe.

If however, the spring is not in a barrel, we must wind it up completely and restrain it within a clamp.

To let down power you will need a letdown key. Select the fitting that is the same size as the winding square. You will hold the letdown key tightly with downward pressure and allow the key to slip through your hand under your control as you release the ratchet click. Make sure the clamp is in the middle of the spring.

With the power let down or clamped, it is now safe to take the movement apart.

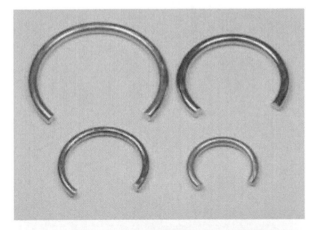

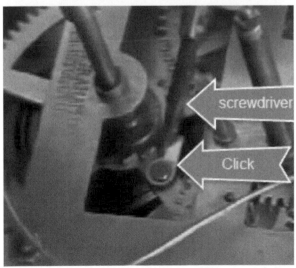

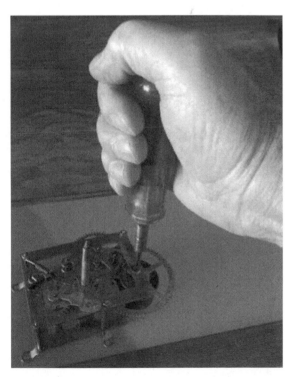

Dismantling the Movement

I strongly recommend you first take apart a junk clock that has little value and no sentimental attachment. The last thing you want to do is damage a family heirloom or an expensive Vienna Regulator. Ideally start with a time-only movement, then move on to a typical American time and strike mantel clock.

Before you start to take anything apart, it is most important that you document the entire movement, step by step. Take good digital photos of the front, sides, and back of the movement [not the case]. Make sure the pictures are sharp, in-focus and all parts can be seen. Also, make a diagram of the front, sides, and back. **Do not skip this step**. Take your time and make it as accurate as possible. Note each wheel and if the pinion is on top [up] as setting on the bench, or on the bottom [down] of the wheel PU or PD. Note the direction of the mainsprings.

This will not only help when putting the movement back together, it will also help you understand the various parts of the movement. The springs and any barrels may look alike but do not get them mixed up. Keep the going and striking parts separate and marked.

If the movement has a striking train, making sure the strike is in the 'lock' position [just after completing striking] and note the position of all pins located on wheels or other places, and any cams, levers, and a rack or cam wheel. When you put it back together again, these all need to be in the same position. Note the name of each wheel [Great wheel, intermediate wheel, hour wheel,

escape wheel etc] and the wheel number – time side is T1, T2, T3 etc with the largest wheel being T1. On the striking side label them S1, S2 etc. [S is for Striking]

The Diagram

Many new students taking their first movement apart are concerned they will not be able to put it back together. Others just jump right in without any study of the movement or documentation.

The best insurance you will successfully get a clock movement back together and run is to properly document the movement. Slow and steady is faster. Having said that, I have seen some pretty sad diagrams that have insufficient information, and others that try to be a work of art, detailing all kinds of irrelevant details.

For this reason, I will give an example of a good and detailed diagram that does not need an artist's skill and has everything you need without any unnecessary clutter.

I will use the following two train movement with count wheel, as an example.

Sometimes the diagrams can start to get so busy it is hard to read. It is a good idea to create several diagrams, each with certain items you want to note.

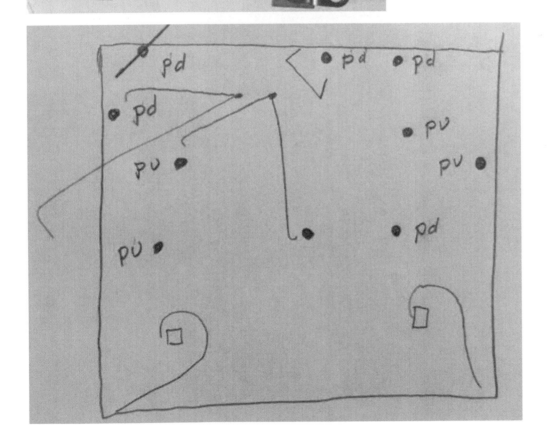

I will first describe the two trains so you can identify each wheel.

Strike Train

I will start with the strike train because each wheel can be identified fairly easily [except the great wheel anyway].

T2 [in this clock] has two pinions. One to drive T3 and one to drive the count wheel.

T3 has a cam attached to it.

T4 is the warn wheel, has the warn pin on it.

T5 is the fly.

Time Train

After identifying the strike train, the remaining time train can most often be identified in size order, the largest being the great wheel and the last wheel being the escape wheel with sharp teeth.

T1 First or Great wheel - is attached and ratcheted to the main spring, or cable, barrel. The ratchet allows the mainspring or cable barrel to be wound without turning the wheel. The ratchet is called "the click". The first wheel turns the pinion of the Center wheel.

T2 Center or second wheel - which turns once per hour. It's pinion is turned by the teeth of the mainspring barrel in spring driven clocks, and by the weight pulley in weight driven clocks. Its arbor projects through a hole in the dial and drives, via a friction coupling, the cannon pinion, which carries the minute hand. It also drives the pinion of the third wheel.

T3 The third wheel - drives the pinion of the fourth wheel.

T4 Fourth wheel - This turns once per minute. The fourth wheel also turns the escape wheel pinion.

T5 Escape wheel - This wheel is released one tooth at a time by the escapement, with each swing of the pendulum. The escape wheel keeps the pendulum swinging by giving it a small push each time it moves forward.

There are couple more wheels. The hour wheel which is very distinctive with the long arbor with a square end for the minute hand, and the minute wheel which is the only wheel with a solid pinion [not a lantern pinion]

The great wheels may well look identical so it is best to scratch an *S* or a *T* on each wheel. On your diagram make sure you indicate which direction the spring travels.

Levers

The one place my students seem to neglect is the diagram and causes the most frustration on reassembly are the levers. Knowing how they fit between the wheels is invaluable. I suggest you spend more time on the levers in your diagram than anything else.

Wire Springs

There are likely several wire springs on your movement. These springs ensure the levers return to the ready position when not operating. Note the location, what it is tensioning and how the spring is anchored to the frame.

Dismantling - Continued

Inspect the movement very closely from the front and the back. Look at each pivot with a loupe or magnifying glass to see if there is any wear / elongated pivot holes. If wear is found, note them on your diagram including the direction of the wear.

Check 'endshake'. Endshake is a small amount of movement between the plates by each wheel. If a wheel were tight between the plates, it would add a lot of friction, so make sure the wheel will move up and down very slightly between the plates. Ideally, endshake should be around 0.010inch. The fact is it can be more than this as long as the wheel does not fall out, the teeth all mesh correctly and any striking pins still do their job.

Hold the movement horizontal, ie with the front plate up. Keeping the movement horizontal, view each wheel to see if they have all dropped down onto the back plate. Then rotate the movement 180 degrees with the back plate up. Check if each wheel has dropped down to the front plate. Any that did not drop on their own have a problem. The barrel needs very little endshake.

Clock movements are held together either by a nut or by tapered pins, usually one in each corner. Remove the nuts or tapered pins and keep them safe.

With the movement horizontal, very slowly remove the upper plate in a way that all the internal wheels and components stay in position. Take another photo inside with the top plate removed, and make another detailed diagram. Make sure you include any levers in your diagram.

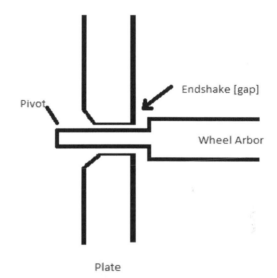

String each train of wheels together in order. You can hang the wire over the edge of the cleaner.

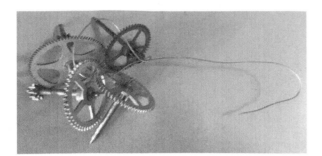

Cleaning the Parts

The cleaning solution can be bought from specialty parts houses or made at home using the following recipe:

4 oz. oleic acid [Use Murphy's Oil Soap]
8 oz. Acetone
12 oz. 26% Ammonium Hydroxide
1 Gallon Water
Let soak for 5 minutes then scrub the parts with an old toothbrush.

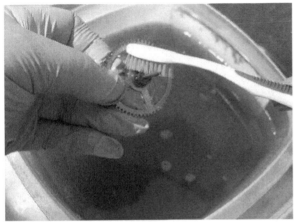

My personal preference is "Polychem Deox-007 Concentrate" it has no nasty ammonia odor and one gallon makes eight gallons of cleaning solution.

⁕ A mildly alkaline blend for the efficient removal of oils, grease, tarnish, stains, corrosion, and oxidation from brass, bronze, copper, gold and silver
⁕ Can be safely used in ultrasonics, agitated tanks or manually
⁕ Provides long-term protection from tarnish, corrosion, and oxidation
⁕ Removes tarnishes and brightens metal parts
⁕ Use with water in a 7:1 water/concentrate ratio
⁕ No strong odor
⁕ Nonhazardous

The gold standard for cleaning movements and parts is an ultrasonic cleaner.

It is the same device that the health industry uses to sterilize surgical instruments. An ultrasonic cleaning is a process that uses ultrasound and an appropriate cleaning solvent. They can be spendy.

You can buy a jewelry ultrasonic cleaner much cheaper but make sure it is big enough to fit the movement plates and pillars and all the wheels.

I string the wheels together for each train on a thin wire and drape the end over the side of the tank. Saves having to fish the parts out when done. Use a tea bag strainer for screws and small parts.

For extra dirty movements or parts, protect your cleaning solution by pre-cleaning. Carb or Brake cleaner which is mostly acetone works great and the pressurized spray helps blow away the residue. Best if you use the straw.

Plan on cleaning the movement as soon as you have taken the movement apart so you can fully evaluate the parts for wear and defects.

Once the movement servicing has been completed and immediately before final assembly, clean the parts again. Once clean, use gloves to handle the parts so the oils from your hands don't tarnish the bright parts.

It is a good idea to have two batches of cleaner going. Use the older cleaner to do the first wash which will discolor the solution. Use the freshest solution for the final wash. Eventually, this will become the first wash and new solution will become the final wash.

Scratch Brush

If you have parts that are very dirty, in places that are hard to reach or have tarnish or minor rust, you can use a Scratch Brush, which is an inexpensive tool that contains a fiberglass cartridge that does a good job of cleaning this difficult tasks.

Drying after Cleaning

After immersing your parts in the cleaning solution, the next step is to rinse all the solution off the parts with clean warm water. When complete, ALL moisture must be removed from the parts or they will start to rust. This is easier said than done. The most common method is to create a simple heat box. It could be cardboard or a plastic container with a lid. Cut a hole in the top just large enough for a hair dryer nozzle to fit through. Also, make some holes near the bottom for cooler air to escape.

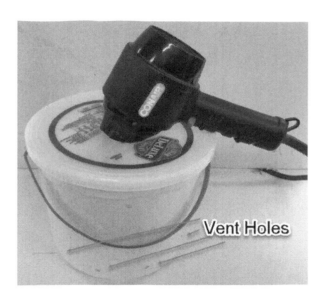

With the parts inside the box, run the hair dryer on hot for about 10 or 15 minutes. When removing the parts, they will likely be quite hot so let them cool before handling them.

Pegging

Commercially available peg wood is either orange wood or dogwood but good quality round toothpicks will work in a pinch. Pegwood is generally used to remove any residual chemicals or oils from inside the brass pivot holes but can also be used as a burnisher to smoothen and harden the hole.

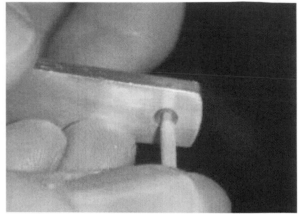

To use peg wood as a burnisher, hold it in a lathe, cordless drill or Dremel tool, and spin at a fairly high speed. When turned at high speed in a pivot hole, the peg wood will squeak as it burnishes the pivot hole and actually becomes burnished itself. Burnish from both sides of the plate, and replace or reshape the peg wood when discolored.

Using toothpicks as peg wood is faster, easier, and more cost-effective since there is no need to carve them to shape and toothpicks are very inexpensive. When burnishing, the toothpick will compress and even become dense enough to burnish the inside of the plate hole. And when the toothpick gets worn beyond use, throw it away and use another.

Use peg wood with a chisel shaped end to clean the pinions.

Making Repairs

The first job is to check the wheels one by one, especially noting any wear on the pivots.

The pivot should be perfectly cylindrical in shape. After wiping and cleaning the pivot with pith wood, it should have a visibly smooth surface. Slide your fingernail over the pivot. It should slip along the surface, and there should be no grooves or roughness perceptible to the touch. Inspect the pivot using a loupe [or strong magnifying glass] looking for defects. **It should have a mirror finish.** Place your fingernail up against the pivot, you should see a reflection.

Note: the pivots must be corrected **before** pivots holes are corrected [bushed] because dressing a pivot will tend to reduce its diameter very slightly.

My homemade portable lathe consists of a Ryobi cordless drill, clamped to my bench and a second clamp to hold the trigger down while I use the drill. The keyless chuck is accurate enough for all but the most delicate clocks.

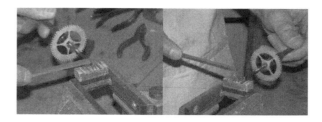

I made my own Emery Buff sticks by gluing wet and dry sand paper to tongue depressors in the grades of 600, 1,500 and 2,500. Lay out 4 or 5 tongue depressors side by side, spray with contact cement on the sticks and on a piece of wet and dry sandpaper and glue them together. Use a different grit on the other side. Cut apart when dry. Don't wrap the sand paper around one stick or you won't get the clean square corners that you need.

Only use the very course sticks for badly worn pivots and quickly move up the finer grades ending with the 2,500 grade for a very fine and smooth pivot. Finish with a semi-chrome polishing compound.

The drawback of this system is the abrasive sticks will tend to leave particles of abrasive embedded in the surface of a pivot that can damage the metals if allowed to remain. Make sure you put the parts in the cleaning machine after polishing.

A better solution for high-end clocks is to use a pivot file and a spot of lubricant. A pivot file is designed for the sole purpose of dressing hard tool steel pivots. The teeth are

of extremely fine cut and the file is much thicker than any other of its size. The file will not bend when in use and the edge is offset so you can get right to the root of the pivot.

Once the pivot is flat and true, use a carbide burnisher to work harden the pivot.

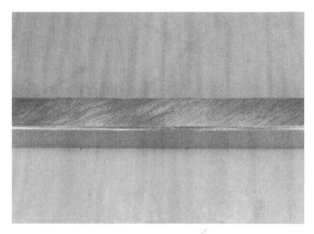

Lubricate it and with the lathe [or drill], turning very slowly, begin to rub the pivot with the burnisher from underneath so you can see what you are doing. Make sure you keep it flat on the pivot so you don't change its shape. The accumulation of black particles forming on the surface of the burnisher will tell if you have applied the burnisher to the work flat against the length of the pivot. As with a file, run the burnisher over the pivot for the full length of the burnisher.

Apply as much pressure with the burnisher as you are comfortable with. Pressure is good, but when a pivot is unsupported, it is possible to break a pivot using unreasonable force. A well-sharpened burnisher does two things. It cuts some metal away and is actually acting as a super-fine file. At the same time, it is compressing the surface of the metal to harden it.

As the pivot is being restored to shape using the coarse side of the burnisher, long, slow, deliberate strokes work best at between 500 and 750 rpm. Once the pivot looks acceptable, wipe the pivot and finish with the smooth side of the burnisher using more rapid, lighter-pressure strokes. Move the burnisher faster, but do not appreciably speed up the lathe. Give the burnisher time to do its job, in other words.

An alternative is a 1/8" x 1/8" x 2-1/2" hard Arkansas stone with lubrication.

If a pivot is badly grooved, removing all the groves may remove too much material, weakening the pivot. In this case, I suggest you just soften up the groves which will do little harm, reduce friction and help hold the oil. However, you should focus your attention on the pivot hole to find the cause of the groves.

It is important to polish the pivot shoulder also.

I often get asked how to hold an arbor in a lathe when the wheel or pinion is so close to the pivot there is no way to chuck up on the arbor. First of all, never chuck up on the pivot [unless you are straightening the pivot – see below]. The simplest answer is to cut a thin strip of fine wet and dry sandpaper and run it around the pivot with your hands.

The correct answer is by using a Jacot Tool. Below are two homemade units. The wheel is fitted in a hole in the end of the Jacot Tool and the other end supported by a steady-rest. The wheel is propelled by the bent metal bar that drives the wheel arm.

My Jacot tool

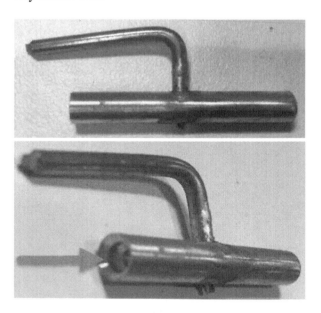

¼" brass rod that has a bent metal carrier [a nail] drilled and soldered into it, with a cone shaped hole in the end to accept the pivot.

Polishing and Burnishing Pivots and Pivot Holes

Burnishing is a combination of polishing and work-hardening of the surface of the metal. The smoother and harder the bearing surfaces, the less the friction and the longer they will function well.

Polishing

Polishing can be performed by any kind of cutting or abrasive device. Polishing powders, diamond compounds, stones, sandpaper, files are common.

A pivot file is most suitable for its ability to true up defects in the pivot such as barrel, bowed, tapered or cone shape as well as pits and grooves. The pivot file should be lubricated with the same or compatible oil as will be used to lubricate the completed movement to draw away shavings. Much practice is needed to develop the correct speed and pressure to obtain the finest finish. Inspect your work with high magnification. Use a back-lit micrometer to reveal defects in the shape.

With the wheel safely mounted in the lathe, bring the pivot file to the work carefully and purposefully from underneath so you can see the pivot at all times. Watch the pattern in the lubricant to determine where the file is contacting the pivot.

Burnishing

A steel burnisher when new needs to be dressed to make the surface flat and free of defects and the surface scored so it will perform its function. To score the flat surface, place fine [150] emery paper on a small sheet of thick glass and slide the steel across and back, creating a series of fine scratches, making it into a micro file. Make one side coarse and the other side fine. Burnish the pivot using light oil at high speed about 2,000 rpm to a black shine.

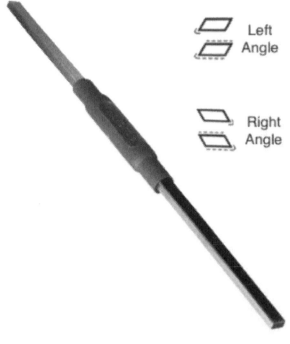

Burnishing the pivot hole

Burnishing the pivot hole is just as important as burnishing the pivot. Use a smoothing broach.

This is a round, tapered steel rod which needs the same prep as the flat burnisher. Fit the broach in the lathe, smooth it with 600 grit sandpaper followed by 0000 steel wool.

After pegging and installing any needed bushings, hand burnish the pivot holes with the prepped and lubricated smoothing broach from both sides of the plate using a light touch. When complete, remove any lubricant and closely inspect the back-lit pivot hole to be sure 100% of the bearing surface is shiny and bright.

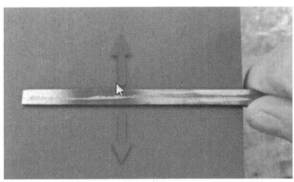

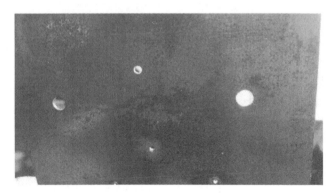

Use this lubricated burnisher the same way you polish as above, closely inspecting your work frequently and critically. Practice and practice. Not enough pressure will not harden the surface. Too much pressure will cause damage. Be sure to burnish the shoulder also as it will also contact the front or back plate. Be sure to remove the burnisher from the work straight down to avoid damaging your work.

The finish you achieve will define you as a craftsman.

Side Bar

My son Jon age 12 came home from Boy Scouts one day with a block of wood and some parts to create a race car for the upcoming Pinewood Derby. This was intended to be a father son project. I was not familiar with this project but did a little research.

The next weekend we sat down to work out our strategy. I told my son the secret of making a winner was the shape of the car; streamline with 2/3rds of the weight at the back, making sure it had the maximum weight allowed. The plan was he would make the car shape in the wood and I would help with the wheels.

An hour later he came back with a design and explained how he arrived at it. He clearly had taken to heart the 2/3rd rule and streamline, so we traced the shape onto the car and I cut out the rough shape on the bandsaw. From there he whittled away and sanded the final shape.

While he was busy doing that, I disappeared into my clock shop and polished up and burnished the axles that held the wheels. I also did my best to burnish the holes in the plastic wheels.

When the car shape was finished, I fitted the axles onto the car and fitted the wheels. My son painted the finished car and we added some lead to bring the weight to the maximum limit.

On the day of the races, the car was inspected by the judge and approved for racing. I added a tiny amount of my best clock oil to each wheel. He won every heat and became the champion in the final.

My son was so proud of the shape he had created and 20 years later he still has that car proudly displayed.

I think he suspects that I had a something to do with its success based on my clock talents.

The morel is of course polishing and burnishing the axles and wheels made a big difference and it will help you clock work just the same.

For a bent arbor, place the arbor on a bench block and rotate it until the high spot is at the top and lightly tap it down with a punch until straight.

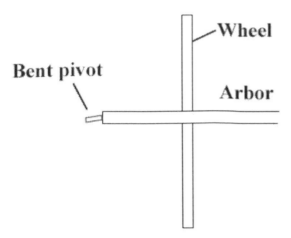

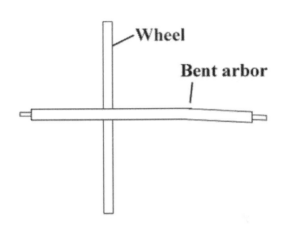

When you come across a bent pivot, you need to very carefully straighten it, hopefully without breaking it off.

Place the pivot in a collet in a lathe. Manually, (BY Hand) turn head headstock. You will be able to observe the wobble. The high point and the low point.

With a peening end of a light hammer, gently tap the arbor to true it. Rotate it so the high spot is on top and gently tap in a very gentle down stroke. This method will work with hard or soft pivots. This task can also be performed vertically on a drill press.

Be forewarned, it takes a learned touch and very gentle taps.

Another way, but this really takes some skill, is to run the lathe at a very high speed and tap downward. You will be hitting the high spot. A series of gentle taps and all of a sudden you will see the arbor/pivot running dead true.

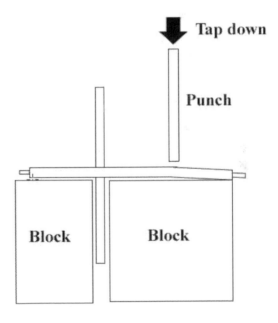

From time to time, you will come across a badly worn or broken pivot. The only solution is to replace the pivot [or replace the whole arbor]. This is surprisingly a straightforward process, one that I enjoy, but it does require the use of a lathe [or drill/Dremel setup], a set of small drills and an assortment of pivot wire. Most likely the original pivot was formed by reducing the arbor diameter from a solid piece of material.

Typically the broken pivot leaves a bump that must be removed "dressed up" so the end of the arbor is flat. Chuck a Dremel cutoff wheel in the lathe and hold the end of the arbor to the wheel until flat.

Chuck the wheel arbor in the lathe and chuck a drill bit in the tailstock. Use a drill one size smaller than the replacement pivot wire. Drill the end of the arbor to a depth of about 3 times the pivot diameter. Make sure it is drilled in the dead center of the arbor.

Insert the pivot wire with Loctite 638 *retaining compound* to hold it in place. Cut to length when set and dress up the end and polish the newly exposed pivot.

The new pivot should ideally be tapered a little to ensure a tight fit. Wait overnight before working the new pivot.

Timesavers sells this Staff and Pivot Wire set for $7.50 and they work well for lantern pinions also.

Staff & Pivot Wire 37-Piece Assortment

37 piece assortment of 6" long hardened staff and pivot wire. Diameter ranges from .027" through .152". Made in India.

Base Pricing: $7.50

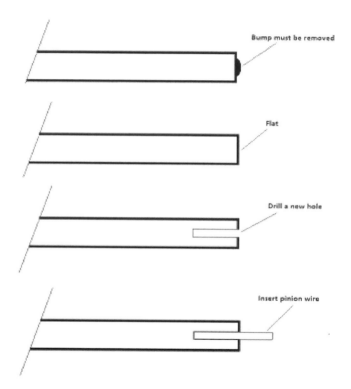

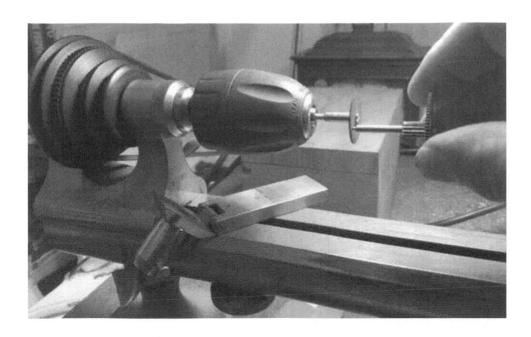

With a dremel cutoff wheel in the lathe chuck, take off any remaining bump off the old pivot.

It is very important you drill the new pivot hole dead center of the arbor. You can use a centering bit [slocombe],

Or better still make your own centering tool.

Use a piece of ¼" brass stock. I prefer to use an octagon shape, but a round profile is just fine. Cut it about ¾" long. Drill a hole down the center using a 1/16" drill bit, then countersink one end. Now you can slide the countersunk end over the arbor. It will automatically find the center of the arbor and use the same 1/16" drill bit to create a small divot in the end of the arbor, dead center. Once you have a divot, you can use the correct size drill bit in a pin vice [or your lathe tail stock] to create the pivot hole.

Keep this drill bit with the tool, they are now one tool. Only use this drill bit for making a center divot with the tool, nothing else.

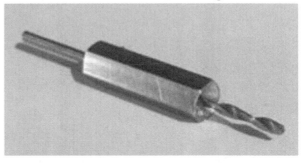

With the wheel in the headstock and a drill bit in the tailstock [or pin-vice], slowly bring the drill to the arbor and bore a new hole for the replacement pivot. Don't add any oil to the drill bit as it will interfere with the adhesive when we install the pivot wire.

You can use any of these Loctite products to hold the pivot. Clean the hole with alcohol before inserting the pivot.

Product Lists by Feature or Application	Top Products by Feature or Application
▸ Fast Cure	▸ LOCTITE® 639 ™ Retaining Compound
▸ High Temperature	▸ LOCTITE® 640 ™ Retaining Compound
▸ High Strength	▸ LOCTITE® 648 ™ Retaining Compound
▸ Close-Fitting Parts	▸ LOCTITE® 603 ™ Retaining Compound
▸ Loose-Fitting Parts	▸ LOCTITE® 680 ™ Retaining Compound
▸ Machinery Repair	▸ LOCTITE® 660 ™ Retaining Compound

Pivoting a Practice Nail

This is a 2 ½" finish nail. I used this because it is soft, cheap, easy to find and easy to work with.

I chucked it up in a lathe [or you could use a dremel] and used my centering tool, just with hand pressure to find the dead center of the end of the nail head.

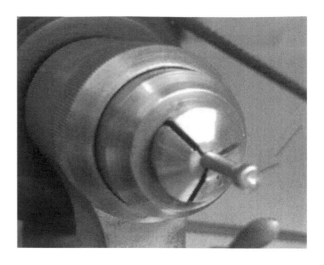

I put a drill bit in the tailstock but it could be in a hand held pin vise.

After drilling the hole, I inserted a taper pin. I probably would not use a taper pin for a real repair but it uses parts you will likely have to hand for your practice.

When you need to bush a clock, it can be done either by hand or with a bushing machine. A bushing machine will cost about $900 and if you have access to one, feel free to use it, but I can bush a clock just as quickly and just as well by hand without the machine.

The following explains the procedure by hand.

What starts out as a round hole, becomes pear-shaped. As a pinion drives the next wheel, it presses that wheel's pivot against the opposite side of its pivot hole. That's where the wear takes place.

You can see where the wear is, just by looking at the pivot hole. It's a good idea to use a marker to indicate where the wear points are, before disassembling the movement. A good rule is if the pivot moves more that the thickness of the suspension spring, it needs repair.

When a gear train is turning in its normal

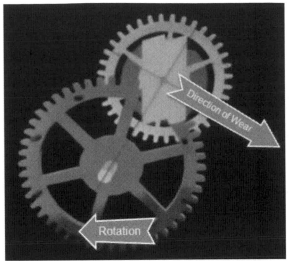

direction, each of its pivots will be pressed against the wear point of its pivot hole.

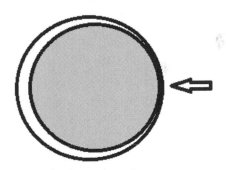

A well made pivot only makes a small contact with its pivot hole

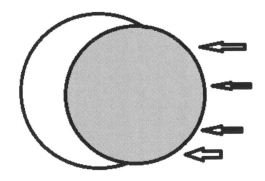

A worn piot hole makes much more contact with its pivot

If one pivot hole is worn, the other pivot will be out of alignment and will bind on its pivot hole.

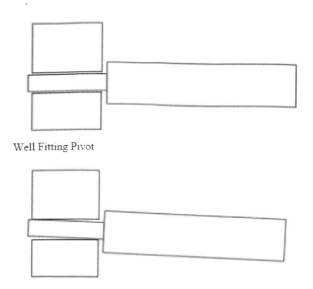

Well Fitting Pivot

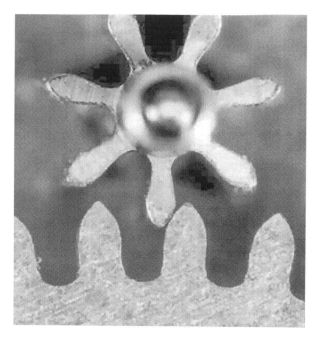

Worn pivot at the other plate causing binding

A worn pivot will also change the mesh [depthing] of the wheel teeth to the pinion.

Mesh too shallow

The challenge is to install a new bushing with the same center as the **original hole**. The first step is to change the pear-shaped hole into a symmetrical oval.

AMOUNT TO REMOVE WITH FILE

Correct mesh

Determine [by eyeball] where the center of the original circle was.

WORN PIVOT HOLE

AFTER FILING

With a small round needle file or Dremel, create an opposite oval identical with and exactly opposite the original oval, until you have an oval hole centered on the center of the original round hole.

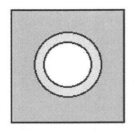

BROACH TO FIT PIVOT

With a cutting broach, broach the hole from the inside of the plate until it is round. A broach automatically centers itself in the middle of an oval. Since that is where the center of the original hole was, the broached hole is still centered on that point.

Continue broaching until the hole is not quite big enough to accept a bushing as a tight force fit. Make sure to keep the broach at a right angle to the plate, in both dimensions, so the hole is straight through.

Select a new bushing that is the same thickness as the plate and has an internal hole just smaller than the pivot.

Use an **oiled** reamer that is made to fit that bushing, cut the hole to final size.

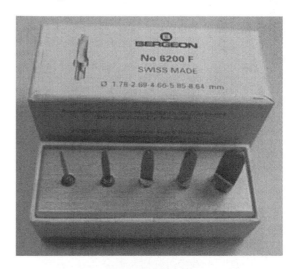

The reamer is a half circle cutter, sharp on both edges, and gets gradually larger as you cut and press on the tool until you get to the parallel portion which is the correct size for a friction fit for the corresponding bushing [3/1000th smaller than the pivot].

Lightly remove any burs with a countersink bit then install the bushing into the hole, from the inside of the plate with the oil sink on the outside, until it is flush with the inside of the plate. Use a small hammer and punch on an anvil block and tap it into place.

Broach and smooth the inside hole of the bush to fit the pivot. Allow 5 degrees of play.

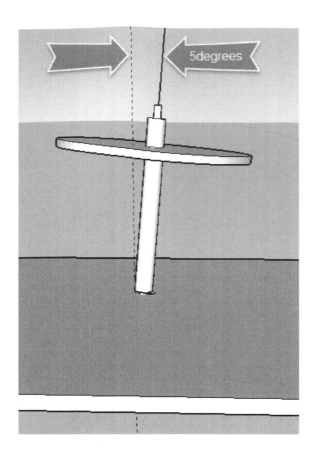

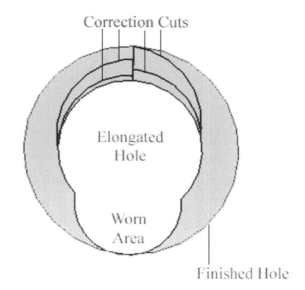

Reaming out the hole will likely leave a burr on the plate. Remove this burr by gently rotating a chamfer tool two rotations.

With the plate supported from the back, lay the new bushing on the hole from the inside of the plate and drive it into place using a punch or brass hammer. Smooth the bushing with emery paper so it is flush with the plate.

Use a Dremel bit #100 in a pin vise to recess the oil sink correctly to correct the double groove shown.

Alternatively, if you just use a reamer instead of a file, make sure you ream out the hole centered on the original hole instead of the new oval. Insert the reamer with the round edge facing the side that is worn. Rotate the cutter ¼ turn left and back to the starting position, then ¼ turn right and back to the starting position. Repeat until the cut area is equal to the worn area, then continue cutting by making full rotations until you reach the parallel portion of the reamer.

This is a good example of marking the pivot holes that need bushing. The point of the masking tape indicates clearly the direction of wear.

Some say you must use a bushing machine to make sure the bushing is fitted perfectly vertical. I am not convinced of this. The final broaching is what must be perfectly vertical.

The main advantage of the bushing machine is you can lock the plate to be exactly in line with the correct location of the pivot hole, not the worn location. Start by loosely fitting the plate in the clamps with the oil sink facing down and the inside of the plate facing up, insert a centering point in the chuck, bring down the point and adjust the plate so it lines up exactly with original pivot hole with the centering point.

Now lock in the clamps.

If the pivot hole is worn oval, align the centering point with the center of the original pivot hole [not the oval], and lock everything down tight.

Next, insert the reamer in the chuck of the tool, add some oil to assist the cutting and rotating it slowly by hand. Bring it down to cut a hole for the new bushing.

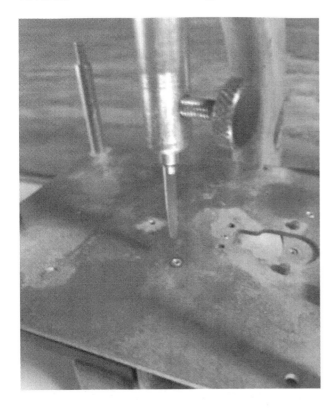

Finally, the hole in the new bushing must be hand opened up using a cutting broach to suit the polished pivot and burnished with an oiled smoothing broach.

Next lightly use the chamfering cutter to take off any sharp edge. Place the correct bush in line with the hole, insert the pusher in the chuck and tap the bushing into place with light taps of the clockmaker's hammer.

Steel Plates

Steel plates are very hard on reamers. I suggest you predrill the holes just under size and finish with the right reamer. Use some cutting oil on the reamer, this saves wear and tear on reamers. Use them only for the final few thou. if at all.

Reamers can be redressed with a fine Arkansas stone. Put the flat of the reamer down on the stone and use a light machine oil on the stone. Hold the reamer down firmly and work it back and forth a few strokes. That way the cutting edge is honed without reducing the OD. This can be done many times without any degradation in performance.

Benchtop Drill Press

An interesting alternative to a bushing machine is a small bench drill press and vice. You can do just about everything a bushing machine will do and a lot more with this setup for under $100. *Timesavers 10305* This one is only 12" tall with variable speed.

There is a Drill Press Bushing Tool Adapter available at Timesavers. A bit spendy.

Capture the clock plate with a 6-Inch Drill Press Vise, which can bolt to the base of the drill press or clamp it down to a piece of backing wood.

With the drill press method, I prefer to open up the pivot hole with a drill bit just smaller than the reamer, then finish up the hole with the reamer. This saves wear on the reamers.

This setup has many other uses including pivot polishing. Lay it on its side and you have a lathe.

Making your own bushings

It is quite easy to make your own bushings in the lathe from common 1/8" brass rod, available from many good hardware stores.

Chuck up the rod in a collet with about ½" protruding. Face off the end, find the center of the end of the rod with your centering bit or homemade tool.

Drill the center hole just a little smaller than the finished pivot, about ¼" deep, with the drill bit held loosely in a pin vise. In the event the bit grabs, let the pin vise spin freely in your fingers until you can shut off the lathe. This technique will save many broken small drill bits.

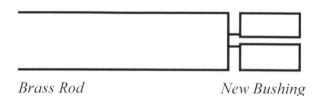

Brass Rod   *New Bushing*

Part [cut] the new bushing to length, just a fraction long. Do not part it all the way off just yet. Remove the rod and bushing from the collet and turn it around so the newly formed bushing is held in the collet. Snap off the extra rod, face up the raw end and chamfer the hole very slightly.

Slip a toothpick into the hole and release the bushing from the collet.

Drill a hole in the plate one drill size smaller than 1/8", dead center on the location of the original pivot center. Broach the hole until the new bushing just starts to enter the hole.

Slip the new bushing into the hole. Lay the plate, outside face up, on a heavy bench block and using a round face punch, give it a sharp

hammer stroke. This will lock the bushing to the plate and create an oil sink all in one process.

Merritt's also sells bushing wire. Long tubes in various diameters which can be more economical than buying individual bushings.

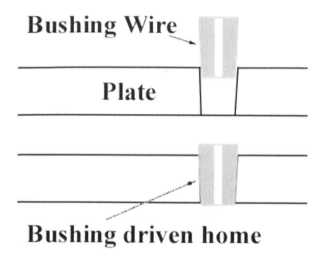

Bushing Wire

Plate

Bushing driven home

For the record, pre-made bushings are available in two grades, Bronze and Brass. Bronze bushings are more durable than brass, however, try to match the same material to the existing plates for fine clocks.

From time to time, you will come across [or create] a broken tooth.

To repair a broken tooth, use a jewelers saw with a very fine 2" long blade, to cut out a dovetail shaped key half way into the rim.

Cut a piece of 1/16" thick 'clock making brass "C-353" extra-long to fit tightly into the dovetail shaped key. Other types of brass might work but they will be harder to cut and fit the exact shape. When in place, lightly hammer the piece on an anvil to slightly rivet and lock it in place. Make sure the cutout and brass replacement is very clean and solder the part in place using 'Tix' liquid flux [not anti-flux] and 'Tix' brand solder using an alcohol lamp. This solder is very hard when set and will withstand the forces acting on the new tooth.

Cut the tooth to length

Slowly file the tooth to the correct profile frequently testing its mesh with the matching pinion between the plates. Use a barrette file with a "safe edge" [an edge without a file profile] so you don't file unintended areas.

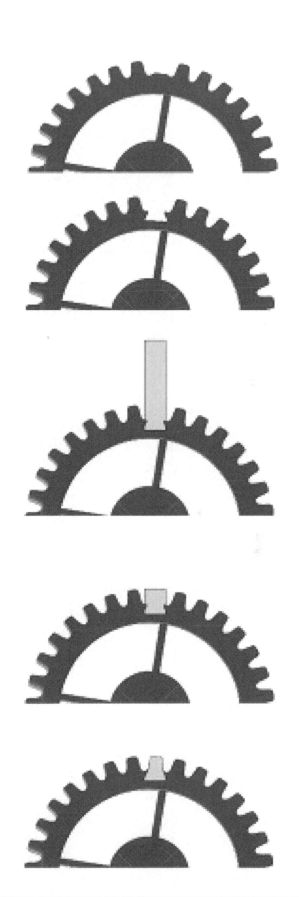

For mainspring barrel teeth repair, you will need to cut out more material as shown.

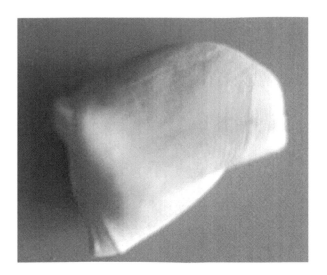

Rodico is available from TimeSavers for $5.00

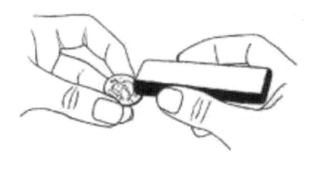

Rodico Cleaner

Description: Single 3" long piece of Rodico for cleaning precision parts, balance pivots, train wheel pivots, or for removing fingerprints and stains from plates, bridges, dials and hands. From Switzerland.

Item #: 14330

Rodico has many uses in clock repair including picking up very small parts safely. In this case, I pressed some Rodico into the wheel that needs a tooth replaced, then used the imprint to make sure the repaired tooth is perfectly profiled.

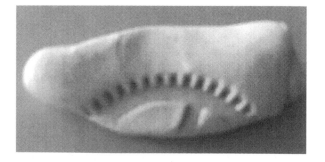

Barrette files

Barrette files are machinist's files that are easily identified by the fact they are only cut on one face, meaning there is a large, safe surface that is referred to as the 'back' [see pointer]. This means only one part of the file can cut a workpiece, leading to a great degree of security against mistakes.

Barrette files usually have trapezoid cross sections, but sometimes they may be triangular, and taper in both width and thickness, which allows them to access small spaces.

They are double cut, but only on the flat face. The uncut face is referred to as the 'back'. This means that they can be used for filing keyways, internal angles in slots and for general finishing and deburring, without fear of accidental wear to another surface during the filing process.

When combined with their taper, the fact that only one of their faces is cut makes them perfect for precision filing.

The Coarseness Rating ranges from #00 the coarsest, to #6 the finest.

To clean any file, rub a piece of copper over it. An offcut of copper pipe is just fine. Copper is soft enough to form grooves in it the shape of the file grooves, which then clean out the file grooves.

A lantern pinion consists of two end caps called shrouds, with hard metal rods or pins called trundles fitted around in a circle creating a very efficient and cost-effective pinion.

It can often be found that these rods are worn, bent, broken or missing.

It is not hard to replace the rods, but I recommend you do not take the whole thing apart at one time. They can be very difficult to get back together again. Rather, replace each trundle one at a time as needed and the job is quite easy.

To replace one trundle, take a small drill bit, about #55 [0.052"] fitted in a pin vice and turn it by hand in the end hole to release the brass that is riveting it in place. It only takes a few turns to remove the soft brass.

Once it is released, you can slide the trundle out using needle nose pliers.

Find a pivot wire that is the correct size, cut it to length, leaving room to rivet [swage] it back in and close the hole a little with a small punch.

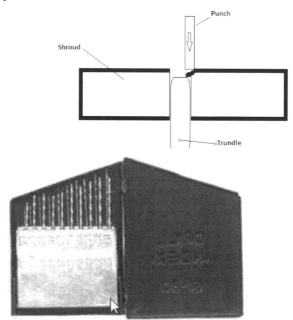

Timesavers sells this drill bit set for $6.50 and they work well for many repair projects including re-pivoting.

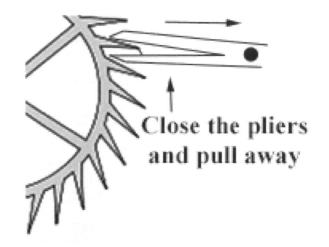

Close the pliers and pull away

Using a good pair of pliers with smooth jaws [no serrations on the inside face] carefully grasp each tooth at the root of the tooth and gently squeezing, 'draw' the pliers out at the correct angle to straighten and stretch the tooth. This needs to be done with great care while the wheel is out of the movement. This will correct any bends and smooth out any imperfections. Every tooth on the escape wheel must be in 'perfect' condition.

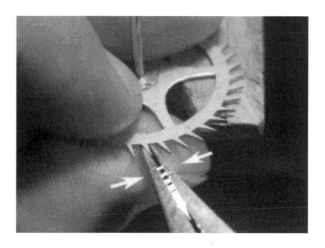

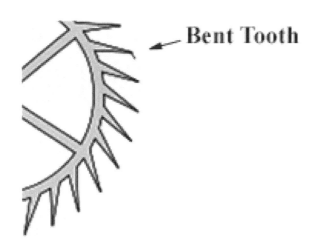

Bent Tooth

After straightening teeth, the wheel will likely need tipping to make sure all teeth are the same length and perfectly round. Use a lathe [or drill] and very light strokes of a file.

After tipping, the backs of the fat teeth will need filing down to between 0.1mm and 0.2mm and make all the spaces between the teeth equal. Create a simple gauge to test the gaps. Press several known good teeth into Rodico to make an impression, then compare this impression to suspect teeth.

Make sure the escapement is properly adjusted. Each tooth should only just clear the pallet. The drop should not exceed 1/6 th the distance between teeth. Check with a feeler gauge. A loud tick or a large drop indicates it is adjusted too far away. Adjust it closer until it catches the tooth, then back it off a fraction until it just clears.

Look closely at the escapement pivots. They should not move from side to side when operating. If it does, the offending pivot hole needs repair.

Motion Work

Motion works

The term motion works refer's to the additional gearing necessary to add a minute wheel/hand. The motion work is the small 12-to-1 reduction gear train that turns the timepiece's hour hand from the minute hand. It is attached to the going train by the friction coupling of the cannon pinion, so the minute and hour hands can be turned independently

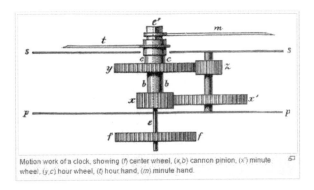

Motion work of a clock, showing (f) center wheel, (x,b) cannon pinion, (x') minute wheel, (y,c) hour wheel, (t) hour hand, (m) minute hand.

to set the timepiece. It is often located on the outside of the movement's front plate, just under the dial.

It consists of:

Cannon pinion- a pinion with a hollow shaft that fits friction tight over the center wheel shaft, projects through the face, and holds the minute hand. While the timepiece is not being set, this is turned by the center wheel and drives the minute wheel. While being set, it is turned by the setting mechanism, in modern clocks a setting knob on the back of the clock. Setting the hands is done by opening the face and manually pushing the minute hand, which rotated the cannon pinion directly.

Minute wheel- It's pinion drives the hour wheel. During setting, this is driven by the intermediate wheel and it turns both the cannon pinion and the hour wheel, moving the hands.

Hour wheel- which fits over the shaft of the cannon pinion, and whose shaft holds the hour hand. The hour wheel rotates once for every 12 rotations of the cannon pinion/minute hand.

It would be possible to use only two wheels to make the gear reduction but that would leave the minute hand traveling counter clockwise. Not good.

ClickWork

The clickwork is a ratchet used so the user can wind up the clock spring without the arbor being able to spin backward. It consists of a gear, click and spring to keep the click engaged with the gear teeth. It is usually located outside the plates on the front side. It allows you to wind in one direction while keeping the mainspring from unwinding. This is due to the fact that the click makes contact with the ratchet wheel and the ratchet wheel is affixed to the main wheel arbor. It is these clicks and click-springs that will allow you to "unwind" or take the power off the mainspring.

The click holds back a lot of power. When you examine a movement while dismantled, test the click. It should rotate back and forth freely but not be loose. Make sure the spring is in good condition.

When oiling a movement, add a little oil to the click.

If the click is loose, it must be corrected for safety. It might be necessary to remove it and re-install it with a new rivet.

Make a dent with a center punch in the center of the top [big end] of the rivet. Drill the rivet out with a bit just larger than the hole in the wheel. Drill until you just reach the wheel but do not cut the wheel. Now you can punch the remaining rivet out of the wheel, while supported it on a staking block. Clean up the shape of the click with a file as necessary.

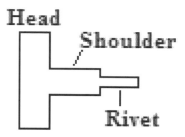

Make a new click rivet on the lathe. The click sits on the shoulder which should be just a fraction bigger than the click so it will rotate smoothly. The rivet goes through the wheel or plate and is riveted over securely on the other side.

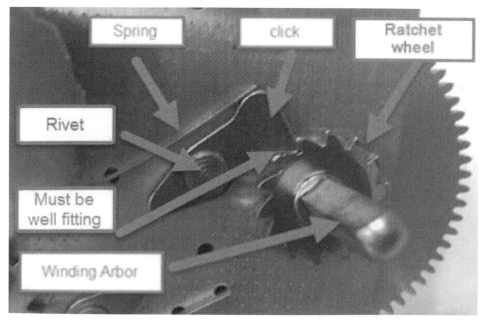

Mainsprings

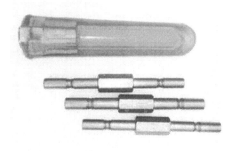

While the movement is dismantled, we need to closely inspect the mainspring to ensure it has not lost its power or worse still broken. At best we need to grease the spring before putting it back into the movement.

In order to inspect the spring, we must first uncoil it and remove it from its wheel. To do this we can use an inexpensive mainspring winder [about $10]. Using this winder, we can release the power under control. It is important you use a thick glove when using this tool to protect your hand.

The winder is placed over the spring with the post [right side] placed through the loop of the spring and the clamp [left side] is tightened onto the edge of the wheel. Holding the spring with the gloved hand, you can wind up the spring enough to remove the C-clamp or wire, release the click and let down the power using a let-down key.

Once the spring has been let down, make a note of the orientation of the arbor on your notes and remove the arbor from the spring. Remove the winder and set the spring on the table.

The spring uncoiled or relaxed should be at least 2 ½ times bigger than when it is would up. If it is not, it is "set" or lost its power and needs to be replaced.

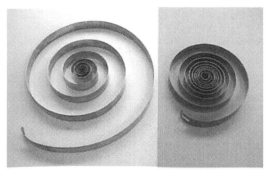

**The spring on the left is new.
The one on the right is old and "set."**

To order a new spring you need to measure the width [½", ¾" etc], thickness [0.013", 0.018" etc], and its length in inches. Then go to the mainspring chart from your parts supplier's catalog. The strength is the thickness of the mainspring and the length is the complete length of the uncoiled mainspring.

Note: new mainsprings, as supplied, are coated with a rust inhibitor rather than a lubricant, and they need to be cleaned and lubricated, before being put into the movement.

If you are interested, the Mainspring Length Formula is:

$$L_{MS} = \frac{1}{2 \times T_{MS}} \times \frac{(\pi \times D_B^2)}{4} \qquad \frac{(\pi \times D_A^2)}{4}$$

where,
L_{MS} is the mainspring length
T_{MS} is the mainspring thickness
D_B is the inside diameter of the barrel
D_A is the outside diameter of the barrel arbor

If the original spring is not broken or set, you can clean the spring and grease it up. Clean it in the regular cleaning solution and dry it thoroughly.

Put the outside end of the spring in a vice and stretch it out [except for the last couple of coils], putting grease on it as you go. I have used 90W, EP gear oil on mainsprings for many years with excellent results. 90W means 90 Weight, and EP means Extreme Pressure. It is commonly available anywhere automotive oils are sold. I use it because I wound numerous mainsprings in a mainspring winder after they were lubricated, and watched the springs uncoil as I slowly unwound them. I concluded that springs with this oil expanded more evenly than ones lubricated with most mainspring greases, particularly within their working range. Use the mainspring winder to put the C-clamp or wire back on.

If your mainspring is contained in a barrel, you can remove it by carefully pulling the center coil out and peeling it out of the barrel. Before taking the cover off, mark the barrel where the cover notch is located so it can go back on in the same location. Also, mark the cover and barrel with an *S* for strike or *T* for time so they go back the same way they came off.

Remove the barrel cover by rapping the arbor on a piece of wood. The cover will pop off. Grasp the two inner coils [the ones closest to the center] with a pair of smooth faced pliers and gently pull the coils out until they are "free" of the barrel. Then slowly and steadily pull the "exposed" coils, by hand, until the mainspring starts to come out.

When several coils are "exposed", grasp the coils with a gloved hand and "guide" the rest of the mainspring out of the barrel. What I mean by guiding is NOT pulling on the spring but a sort of twist and tug which will loosen the coils and the mainspring will almost come out on its own. Please be CAREFUL. This is something that you must "feel" as you go and it takes some practice. Make a note of the orientation of the arbor on your notes and remove the arbor from the spring.

The $10 mainspring winder mentioned above is not ideal for dealing with powerful mainsprings, in fact, some would say this device can be unsafe to use. Besides, it will only work on loop end mainsprings. A better solution is the full-on mainspring winder.

I believe the best winder is the Ollie Baker style mainspring winder. It handles loop-end and hole-end springs, as well as springs in a barrel safely. It utilizes a full set of sturdy sleeves to fit all sizes of springs. Use it with your let down keys and spring clamps.

Reassembly

When the pivots are smooth and the pivot holes are all correct, insert each wheel in place **by itself** between the plates and make sure it spins freely with a little endshake. Test the spin in several positions, top plate up, top plate down, escape wheel up, escape wheel down, looking for any possible interference. It should come to a slow stop, not a sudden stop. Rotating the plates up and down, the wheel should drop onto the other shoulder freely.

When all have been tested individually, insert two at a time to test the mesh of each wheel and pinion. Use only light pressure to feel

any roughness in the mesh at ant point. Then turn them fast to observe them coming to a very gradual stop. When each pair have been tested, insert all the wheels in the **time train only** not including the escapement and test they all spin freely and the teeth mesh correctly on the come to a very gradual stop.

Look for any wobble in any wheel. Do the same for the striking train if the movement has one. If you skip this step, you will likely regret it later.

Next, make a final cleaning and insert everything back into the plates using gloves, without touching the parts with your bare hands. Place the plate that contains the pillars on your box or movement pillars. Refer to your photos, diagrams, and notes. Reset all the wheels and levers in place. Bring the second plate down. One by one using tweezers, locate the top pivots back into their pivot holes. Do not use pliers or anything stronger than tweezers, the pivots can bend or even broken off very easily.

You will find each arbor is a slightly different length. Knowing this, look for the tallest and fit that first, then move on down until you get the shortest.

Typically the great wheel [home to the mainspring] is tallest with its winding arbor. Once this is in place you can usually start a turn of the nuts on the two bottom pillars, then work up the train until you can start a turn on the other two pillar nuts. Each wheel will click in place which I find very satisfying. When the last pivot is located, the upper plate will come down onto the shoulders of the pillars.

This can be a tricky process at first, but it soon becomes easier once you have done it several times and you are more familiar with the parts. Be patient and be prepared that you might have to take the movement apart again and start over if fine tuning is needed. Never force anything and take your time. Make it a habit of testing everything you add during assembly to catch any faults before you get too far. To verify a wheel is in its correct place, using tweezers, slide the arbor up and down. If it is in place it will slide up and down freely. If it is frozen in place, it is trapped between the plates, not in its pivot holes.

Tighten the movement nuts or taper pins and wind the spring a little to remove the spring clamps.

Occasionally you will find that once a wheel is in place and the levers fitted [especially with rack and snail] you can't access the oil

sink. In that case, it is best to oil that pivot during assembly.

Striking Setup

It is important to have a good understanding of the correct striking setup after you put a time and strike movement back together.

After all the wheels are set between the plates, in order for the striking to work correctly and in sync, some adjustments are usually necessary. This explanation is for the more common Count Wheel striking system only.

First, make sure the Count Lever points directly to the center of the count wheel. Adjust it if necessary.

These three items must all be correct at the same time:

- Count Lever in a deep slot.
- Drop Lever must sit in the slot of the Cam.
- Locking Lever must be engaged with the Lock Pin.

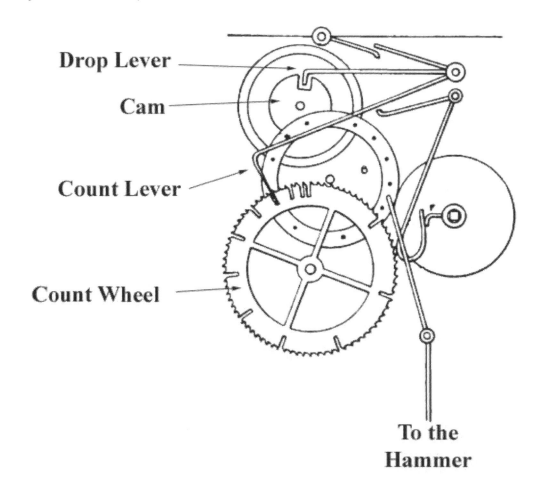

Drop Lever

Cam

Count Lever

Count Wheel

To the Hammer

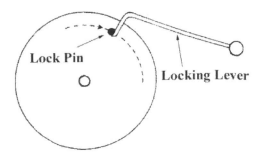

Lock Pin

Locking Lever

If the Locking Lever is not sitting next to the Lock Pin, you may need to open the movement and adjust the meshing of the teeth so it does sit next to the Lock Pin, while the Count Lever is still in a deep slot, and the Drop Lever is still in the Cam slot.

You only want to advance the wheel that is in the incorrect position [usually the locking pin wheel] leaving the rest in the same position. This is easier said than done. To help, press a small amount of Rodico into the wheels you want to stay the same, allowing you to focus on the incorrect wheel. Completely let down the power or capture the mainspring before making any adjustments.

A plate spreader is a very useful tool, allowing you to adjust one wheel without dismantling the complete movement.

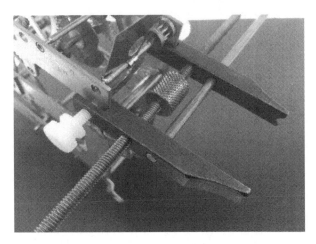

Test it over at least a 24 hour period to make sure everything is working correctly.

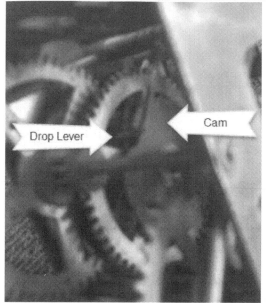

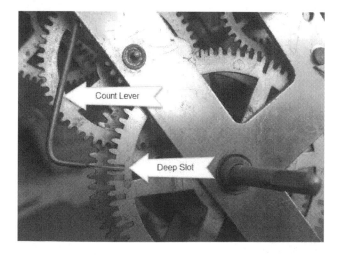

A- Stop Lever

B- Maintenance Lever

C- Count Lever

D- Lift Lever

E- Warning Lever

F- "J" Lever

G- Hammer Lever

H- Stop/Warning Wheel

I- Maintenance Cam

J- 2nd Wheel

K- Count Wheel

L- Strike Release Pins

M- Hammer Detent

N- Hammer

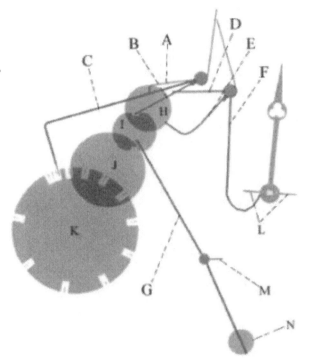

Before you dismantle the movement, look carefully at your movement. You will likely see three sets of levers. Each set is attached to an arbor between the plates.

- Upper Lifting levers
- Lower Lifting levers
- Hammer levers

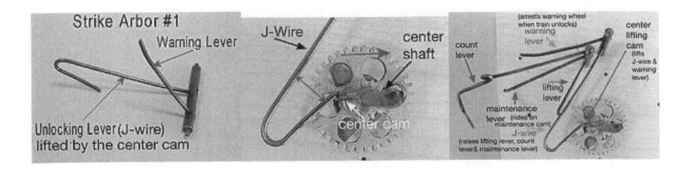

Lower Lifting Levers

Unlocking lever

Warn Stop Lever

J Hook

Upper Lifting Levers

Locking lever

Count Hook

Cam Locking Lever

Count Wheel

Lifting Lever

Hammer

Hammer Levers

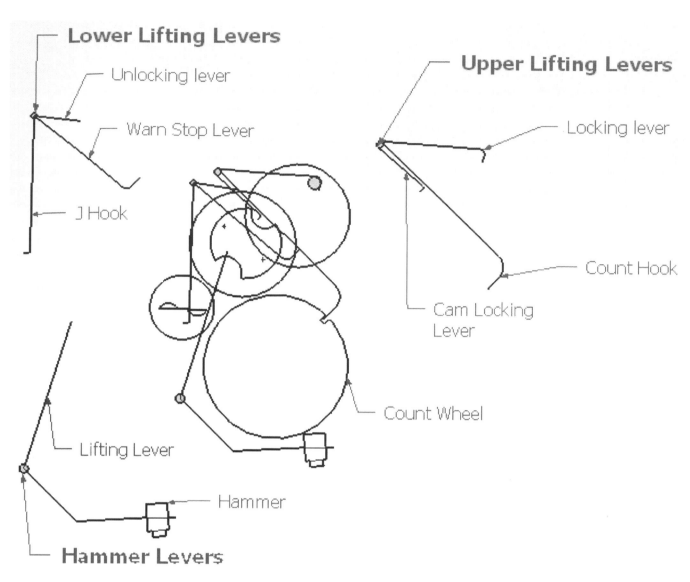

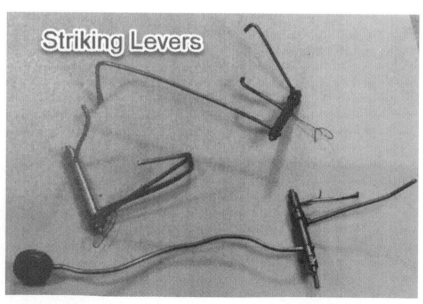

Striking Levers

Rack & Snail Striking

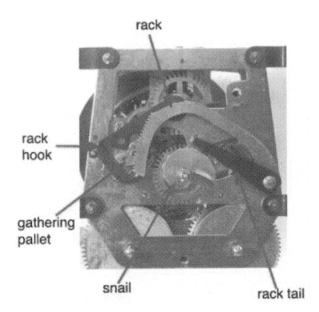

rack

rack hook

gathering pallet

snail

rack tail

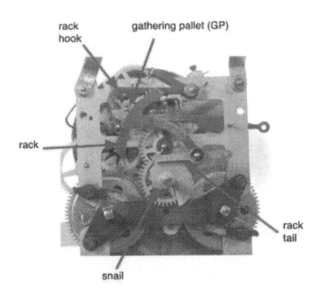

rack hook

gathering pallet (GP)

rack

rack tail

snail

These are two common examples of Rack & Snail striking movements. This is a modern upgrade from the older more primitive count wheel system which is prone to getting out of sync.

The main mechanical components of every rack-striking clock are:

- saw-toothed rack, with a tail
- nautilus-shaped snail, with 12 steps, that turns with the hour hand.
- rack hook, to support the rack
- gathering pallet, to engage the teeth of the rack

The snail with its ever-enlarging radius determines the number to strike and is indexed by the rack tail. The rack counts off the strike.

Things are properly adjusted when...

- When the rack hook is fully dropped beneath the rack,
- The warning pin is resting against the locking stub; and
- The projection on the rack hook is nestled in the dent of the bean cam.

That means the rack hook is synchronized with the warning wheel.

The cam is a pressed fit on its arbor. It can be adjusted either by twisting it on the arbor or by prying it off and repositioning it with its dent against the rack hook pin. Do this while the warning pin is against the locking flag. Observe the position of the pinwheel. There should be a little run before the next pin lifts the hammer.

Identify these parts. Each Rack and Snail striking movement will have some variation on this concept.

The Lift Cam on the minute arbor lifts the Hour Warning Lever.

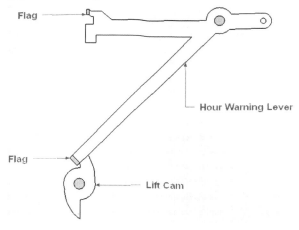

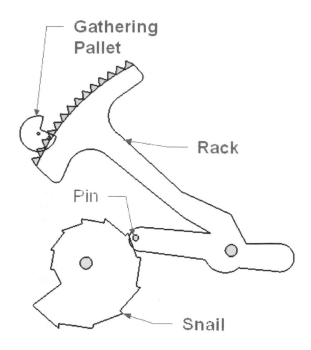

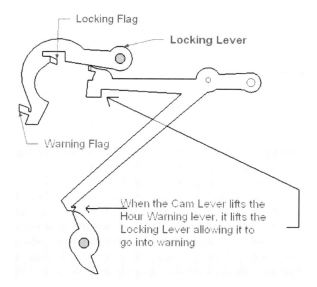

When it goes into warning, the pin on the Rack lands on the Snail to determine how many times to strike. The Gathering Pallet advances the Rack until the correct number of bell or gong strikes have sounded.

Congratulations, you are now **hooked.**

Lubricating the Movement

Lubricants provide a protective film that separates the two rubbing surfaces and reduces the level of friction in the two rubbing surfaces. Correct oiling of the movement is critical. There are many specialty clock oils available which you can use, but there is a motor oil that is ideal. Mobil 1 – 5W-30. Having used this for years, I have found it does not to go gummy and is compatible with the typical clock metals.

A fellow clock repairer used to be a chemist and studied the various clock oils on the market and their viscosity, and recommended Mobile 1 to me.

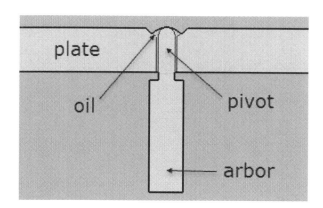

Insert only a small amount of oil in the oil sink. Oil is held in place by capillary attraction and surface tension. If you insert too much oil, the oil will be drawn out and leave it dry.

Ideally use a heavy lubricant for high-torque, low-speed applications [mainspring, 1st and 2nd wheel pivots] like Mobile-1 10W-40, and use a light lubricant for low-torque, high-speed applications [3rd, 4th, escape wheel pivots, balance pivots, escape wheel teeth, clock strike governor pivots, etc.] like Mobile-1 5W-30.

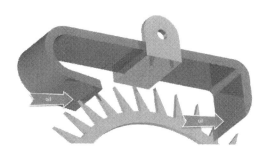

Approximate Viscosities of Common Materials	
Material	Viscosity in Centipoise @70F
Water	1
Milk	3
Nye Clock Oil 140B	20
Sperm Oil	52
SAE 10 Motor Oil	85-140
SAE 20 Motor Oil	140-420
SAE 30 Motor Oil	420-650
SAE 40 Motor Oil	650-900
Mobil 1 5W-30	178
Mobil 1 0W-40	215
Mobil 1 5W-40	250
Mobil 1 10W-40	325
SAE 80W-90	585
SAE 85W140	1750

Place one drop of oil on the escapement pallets impulse face. Do not oil any of the wheel teeth.

Place one drop on each lever post, the minute wheel post and on each click.

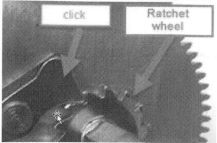

Test Run

Make sure it runs for a full 24 hours before putting the movement back into its case.

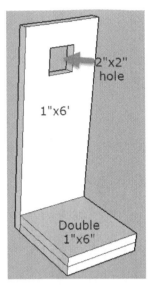

The test stand below fits many movements just sitting on top. It is easy to make using ½" plywood. 12" tall, 8" wide and 6" deep. Cut a hole in the top about 4" by 3" or to suit your movement. The pendulum [and weight chains if it has weights] fit through the hole in the top. Make a second top out of ¼" ply to fit smaller movements. An added front piece will accept movements screwed to its face. Cut a hole in it if needed.

Screw the movement to a [homemade] test stand, clamped to a bench top or table. Make sure it is level to the eye. Add the pendulum, wind it up and start the clock to make sure it runs. Closely observe the movement and listen for all sounds. The tick and tock should be even. Adjust the pendulum crutch if it is not even. Adjust its regulation so it keeps good time.

When I say level, I find my students get paranoid about 'level'. The fact is the movement needs to be held so it is 'in beat' [see the first chapter]. There is no guarantee the movement will be set in the case perfectly level and the place the clock sets might not be perfectly level.

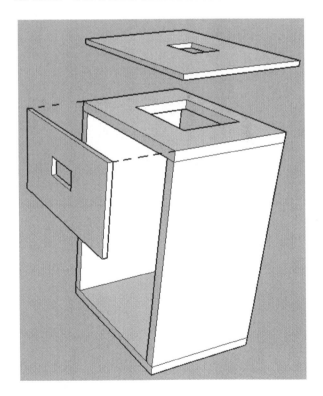

Going Electronic

If we want to get more technical about correctly setting up the beat of a clock, or diagnosing problems, we can introduce some electronic assistance.

The first item is a beat amplifier, available from Timesavers or Radio Shack for under $20, or your clock supply house. Using an alligator clip, attach the amplifier to the mechanism plate and turn it on. It will amplify the tick tock sound making it much easier to get the beat accurately adjusted.

MicroSet

To get more technical, there is the MicroSet which is a digital electronic timer.

It provides unprecedented accuracy, a resolution to a millionth of a second, an optical sensor to eliminate false readings from extraneous noise, and a powerful interface to Macintosh and Windows personal computers. The Count Mode will find the correct rate of any running pendulum clock. The Strike Mode will record the pattern of strikes over many hours to find

intermittent problems. There are also several optional features that can be added.

With this information, you can identify defective escape wheel teeth and put a clock in beat very precisely by reading the digital display.

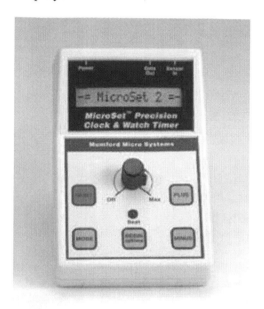

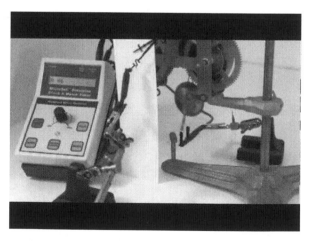

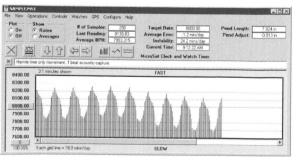

Refinishing the Clock Case

Many of the clock cases you come across are very dirty, often very dark from the years of household furniture polish and normal dust floating in the air and probably smoke. The motto "Do No Harm" means we want to restore the clock back to its original state as close as possible while doing as little damage or alteration as possible.

Start by taking the case apart as much as you can: movement, glass, hardware. Our goal is to remove the dirt and furniture polish back to the original French polish finish underneath.

There are many cleaning products on the market that will remove the dirt, however, most of these products will work too well and damage the original polish below over time. We learn from museum restoration practices that any cleaner with a PH above 7.0 will not only clean as you work on the clock, but will continue to eat at the surface long after you have finished, damaging the original polish or shellac.

My recommendation is to use "Mr. Clean". This product happens to have the perfect PH value at just under 7.0 and removes the dirt with very little effort. Just put some Mr. Clean on #0000 Steel Wood and using light pressure in a circular motion, clean off the dirt. You will likely see the hidden wood grain re-appear.

At this point, using a soft cotton rag and giving a little pressure to rub the surface and generate a little heat to reactivate the shellac. If the original surface has minor damage like scratches, water marks or alligatoring, you can use an "Amalgamator" from Mohawk. Used carefully it will reactivate the shellac a little and blend it to create a newly restored finish.

Any loose veneer can be reglued using "Hide Glue". This is the type of glue used by the original case maker and we still use the modern version from Titebond because it can be unglued using vinegar and re-glued after repairs and restoration had been completed.

Once all the dirt is removed, you need to "Feed" the wood again and for this, it is recommended you use Howard "Feed-n-Wax" orange oil which is readily available. This will stop the pores from completely drying out and give life back to the wood.

The final step is to protect the clock case with Bri-Wax to give a mat shine that resembles the original hand rubbed French Polish.

If the original finish is too badly damaged, use a good quality stripper to remove the old finish. Do not use a water-based stripper or it will likely harm the veneer. Make sure 100% of the old finish is removed. Use gloves and eye protection. Let the stripper sit for at least 15 if not 30 minutes to allow it time to do its work. Repeat the stripper if necessary.

When all the finish is off, wash the case with mineral spirits to remove any residue.

Sand all the bare wood, starting with 300 grit, working up to 800 grit. Wipe clean with a tack cloth.

Staining the case is optional. Some feel it enhances the natural wood grain. I like Minwax. After staining, use #0000 steel wool and wipe clean with an old t-shirt.

Others prefer to see the woods natural color without stain.

Next use a wood filler. Not to fill holes but to fill the wood pores. Wipe on, leave for 15 minutes and buff off with burlap.

Lastly, add a seal coat. Varnish is good but takes days to dry and picks up any and all dust in the air. Do not use Polyurethane.

The best choice is Tung Oil. Plan on 6 to 10 coats, letting each coat dry overnight and rubbing with #0000 steel wool and a t-shirt before applying the next coat. You will be delighted with the finish and it is fool proof.

Anniversary Clocks

The Anniversary Clocks or 400-day clocks are actually called a 'torsion pendulum clock', or torsion clock. It's is a mechanical clock which keeps time with a mechanism called a torsion pendulum. This is a weighted disk or wheel, often a decorative wheel with 3 or 4 chrome balls on ornate spokes, suspended by a thin wire or ribbon called a torsion spring (also known as "suspension spring").

The torsion pendulum rotates about the vertical axis of the wire, twisting it, instead of swinging like an ordinary pendulum. The force of the twisting torsion spring reverses the direction of rotation, so the torsion pendulum oscillates slowly, clockwise and counterclockwise. The clock's gears apply a pulse of torque to the top of the torsion spring with each rotation to keep the wheel going.

The wheel and torsion spring function similarly to a watch's balance wheel and hairspring, as a harmonic oscillator to control the rate of the clock's hands. It is to some degree a different animal, but in many respects, they are very simple to work on. They are simple from the respect that they are time only, with no striking or chiming trains, no levers, and pins.

However setting up the suspension spring requires specialized instructions. For this reason, it is recommended the following book be purchased and studied prior to starting work.

"Horolovar 400 Day Clock Repair Guide"

The movement is generally like any other time and strike movement, with a rack and snail operation. The difference comes outside the plates. There are two bellows at the rear to make the cuckoo sound, operated by wires. These bellows are held to each side of the rear of the case with one screw and brad, and or a spot of glue. To remove them to gain access to the movement, unscrew the screw from outside and pry off the small amount of glue with a small putty knife.

No clock book would be complete without a discussion about Cuckoo Clocks. Some clock people love them and others hate them. The fact is they are not the easiest clock to work on because of the levers setup. Follow along to learn the trick.

The majority of modern cuckoo clock movements are made by Regula. It might not say Regula but if the movement says 25, 34, or 35 on it, it is Regula. It comes in one-day [#25] and eight-day [#34 & #35] wind. You can still buy a replacement Regula movements and parts if needed.

Note, this movement has a replacement bellows on the right.

The bird is attached to a horizontal heavy arm [pearch] with a wire connecting it to the door.

The exact configuration of the wires is critical to the correct operation, so before dismantling anything, make detailed notes, diagrams, and photos. DO NO be tempted to bend any wires. Their shape is critical.

Power comes from pinecone weights on a chain over a great wheel sprocket.

Dismantle, clean and repair the movement just like any other movement as described previously.

Many of the case parts are readily available from the parts houses – carved bird, bellows, pendulum, dial, hands, weights etc.

When removing the movement, remove the hands by unscrewing the handnut, and disconnect the bird from its perch and the door. Close and latch the bird door and lay it on its face. Remove the back door. Disconnect the bellows and remove them down and out to disconnect the wires. Disconnect the chain pull ends and pull the chain off the sprocket and though the case.

Do not remove the hand shaft on the front plate. Because the weight chains and pendulum pass through the case, the movement is exposed to more dust than usual. For this reason, the pivot side shake and end shake are designed looser than usual and badly worn pivot holes are rare. The bellows top [fabric] is fragile and often need replacing.

After cleaning and making any repairs, reinstall in reverse order.

The setup is correct when the last bellow lever has just dropped, the door has closed and there is still a little free spin after warning to lift the gong hammer and then open the door.

Adjust the gathering pallet so the pin is engaged when the lever is sitting midway on one snail step.

My best advice is to obtain a used movement [Regula 25] that has not been dismantled and keep it as a guide to the correct setup [a go-by].

To reinstall the chain, turn the movement upside down. Feed the chain onto the sprockets. Advance the sprocket with your finger and rotate the movement round as it pulls the chain in until it emerges out of the bottom. Tie off the chain so it does not come off while you work on the other chain.

These clips are tricky to remove. Scratches around the clip are a sure indication someone else has worked on the movement before you.

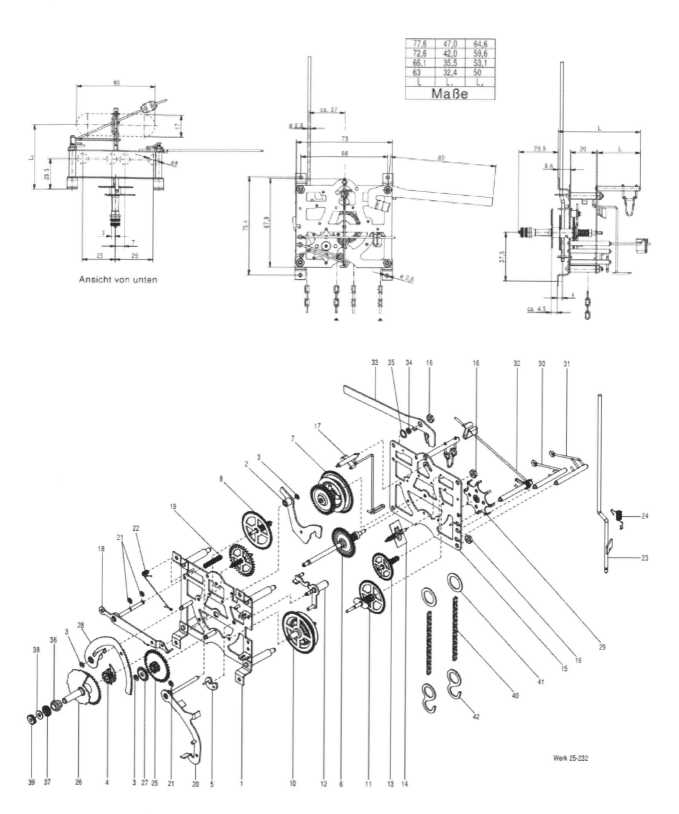

77,6	47,0	64,6
72,6	42,0	59,6
65,1	35,5	53,1
63	32,4	50

Maße

Ansicht von unten

Werk 25-232

Item	Description
1	Rack board
2	Locking lever
3	Safety washer
4	Trigger
5	Gathering pallet
6	Minute wheel shaft
7	Ground wheel gear
8	Center wheel
9	Climb wheel
10	Ground wheel perc.
11	Gathering pallet wheel
12	Release lever
13	Impeller
14	Wing
15	Plate
16	Hex nut
17	Anchor
18	Warning lever
19	Pressure spring
20	Fallen Lever
21	Safety washer
22	Spring for trap
23	Birdstock
24	Birdstock spring
25	Changeover wheel
26	Pointer wheel
27	Washer for change
28	Raking
29	Bearing disc
30	Whistle wave
31	Whistle wave
32	Hammer shaft
33	Shut-off lever
34	Socket
35	Adjusting wheel
36	Pointer socket
37	Pointer socket
38	Disc ø2.6
39	Hand nut
40	Chain 70" long
41	Chain ring
42	Chain hooks

If you buy a clock without a pendulum, you can use the following to calculate the correct length:

Tips on Counting Teeth
With a sharpie, place a dot next to the tooth that you will start counting. Now you will know when to stop counting.

If the wheel is out of the movement, run the wheel across a sheet of paper and count the holes.

Formulae:

$$BPM = \frac{W_E \times W_4 \times W_3 \times W_C}{P_E \times P_4 \times P_3} \times \frac{2}{60} \text{ [5 wheel train]}$$

OR

$$BPM = \frac{W_E \times W_3 \times W_C}{P_E \times P_3} \times \frac{2}{60} \quad \text{[4 wheel train]}$$

$$L_P = \frac{141120}{BPM^2}$$

where,
BPM is beats per minute
W_E is the number of teeth on the escape wheel
W_4 is the number of teeth on the fourth wheel
W_3 is the number of teeth on the third wheel
W_C is the number of teeth on the center wheel or center pinion for a 4 wheel train
P_E is the number of leaves on the escape wheel pinion
P_4 is the number of leaves on the fourth wheel pinion
P_3 is the number of leaves on the third wheel pinion
L_P is the pendulum length

Or, you can make a temporary pendulum using wire or a stick and experiment until it is approximate, then buy a pendulum that length and fine tune it using the rating screw. The size of the clock case is a big clue to the length of the pendulum.

Without going into detail about pendulum design, it should be understood that the standard pendulum rod will expand and contract with temperature, affecting its timekeeping. More expensive clocks have attempted to minimize this with compensating pendulums or various types.

If the Suspension spring is missing

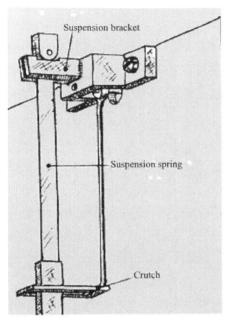

The suspension spring is the flexible transition from the static clock movement to the swinging pendulum. They come in many shapes and sizes.

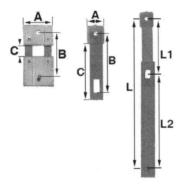

They can be obtained from the usual supply houses, but if the old one is missing, how do you know how long, wide, thick to order?

There is no easy answer. There is no such thing as a chart or book giving the proper length of suspension spring for a particular clock, or simple formula to calculate it out. But you can use the following tips to find a suitable suspension spring.

1. Select a spring with the correct top and bottom attachment.

2. Take the mathematical length of the pendulum and deduct the actual length of the pendulum to determine the missing length. Note, the length of the pendulum is measured from the center of the pendulum bob [in most cases] to the center of the suspension spring [or point of flex].

3. Look for the marks that have been made by the crutch pin, or fork. With everything lined up you can measure, or trial fit, a suspension that will be very close to the old one. The marks will line up.

4. Buy a selection of springs. You will need them eventually.

5. Heavy pendulum, thicker spring, light pendulum, thinner spring

6. Typically, it is desired that the inflection point should be aligned with the arbor for the verge. This would be for minimal friction from sliding where the crutch pushed the pendulum/leader. This is not always done but the better clock maker did design that way. For a loaded spring, the inflection point is a little below the center of the spring. The lighter the spring, the more this goes lower. A thicker or wider spring would also speed up the calculated rate of the pendulum [like making gravity stronger].

A heavy bob is less affected by this parameter than a light one. The inflection point of a spring can be determined by drawing a straight line along the center of the pendulum with the pendulum swung to either side.

If the pendulum does not swing in a straight line, or rolls, a wider spring is indicated.

Watches

I want to say a few words about watch repair.

By far, the majority of hobbyists work on clocks rather than watches. It is my opinion that much more would work on watches if they had a little guidance and encouragement, so I will give a brief introduction here.

The biggest fear about watches is how small the parts are, especially for the more mature adults whose vision is less than stellar. The fact is, with the correct working environment and optical aids, all this can be easily overcome.

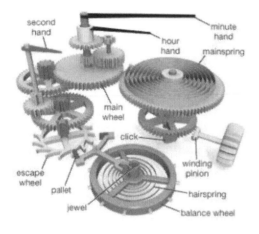

When I was at horological school, we spent time working on watches. At the start of each session, I would set up my workspace with my project and all the tools at hand, quiet with good lighting. I would sit in front of my project for a minute as an "attitude adjustment" period, slowing down my body and mind and gaining a calm peace. I would put on my optical magnification and "climb inside the movement" so to speak and work on the project.

At this point, I will point out the positives of working on watches.

- The process of working on watches is "one item at a time". Stripping down a movement means taking each part off the movement one item at a time in a logical sequence. Even watches with many "complications" [calendar, automatic action, stopwatch, etc.] just means more parts to remove in the sequence. With good notes, everything is very logical.
- The movement is basically "time only", i.e. no additional trains for striking or chiming.
- The movement is usually 30 hour, not 8 days or 30 days, so there are not many wheels.
- As opposed to clocks that have one front plate and one rear plate and as many as 15 wheels and several levers must be fitted **all at the same time**, watches typically have "bridges' that often only contain one, two or three wheels so re-assembly is a breeze.

Here you see the bridge that holds the balance wheel, held by one screw [actually called a cock], then the bridge that holds the mainspring barrel, held by two screws.

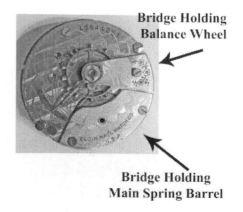

Bridge Holding Balance Wheel

Bridge Holding Main Spring Barrel

Removing the remaining train bridge held by three screws exposes the remaining three wheels.

I recommend first practicing on a pocket watch, ideally an 18 Size Railroad Style Pocket Watch Movement by Elgin. This is one of the largest watches and very easy to work on. Or better still find a "3 finger pocket watch". Each wheel has its own bridge.

There are several good videos on YouTube showing disassembly and reassembly for these watches, and you can usually find them inexpensively on eBay.

Once you have stripped, cleaned and put one back together, you will find working on all other watches is very similar and straightforward. Watch some YouTube videos. Find a good book on watch repair like "Practical Watch Repairing" by Donald De Carl. Give it a try.

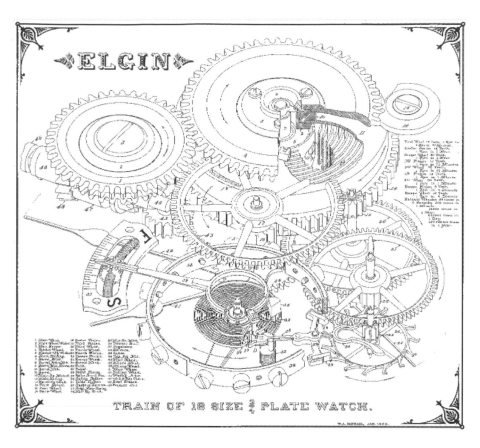

TRAIN OF 18 SIZE ¾ PLATE WATCH.

The Lathe

Why a lathe?

One of the most expensive ~~toys~~ tools we use is a jeweler's lathe. However, used lathes are often available on eBay for a few hundred dollars.

I am going to give a general description of a lathe and what it is used for.

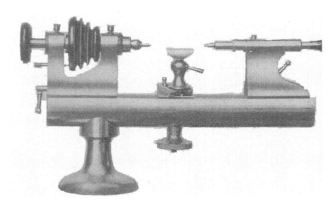

A jewelers' lathe is a small lathe suited to clock and watch repair. It consists of a:
Bed – the general base and horizontal support
Headstock – holds and drives the work
Tailstock – can support the end of the work or hold tools
Tool rest – to support tools that do the cutting
Motor – to drive the headstock using a belt and controlled by a foot switch
Cutting tools – gravers, drills, files etc

Lathes come in different sizes. 8mm is most common but some use a 10mm size. The size refers to the size of collet it takes.

The 'work' is most commonly held in a collet rather than a chuck.

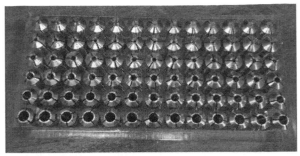

Collets come in sets and the work is held in the collet the same size as the work it holds. This set is 3 to 80 with no gaps. set of 8mm A good beginner set of collets could consists of:
10, 12, 14, 16, 20, 25, 30, 35, 40, 45, 50
and this will cover most items.

It is important the correct size collet is used as described below.

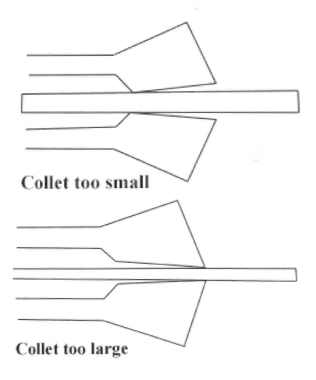

Collet too small

Collet too large

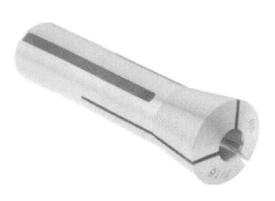

The collet must be the same internal diameter as the work it holds, so it grips the work its entire length keeping the material very stable.

If the collet is too small or too large, the inside of the workpiece can be unstable and wobble making the cut inaccurate. It might mark the work also where it grips.

It is nice to have a way to hold drill bits - either collets or small jacobs chuck in the tailstock.

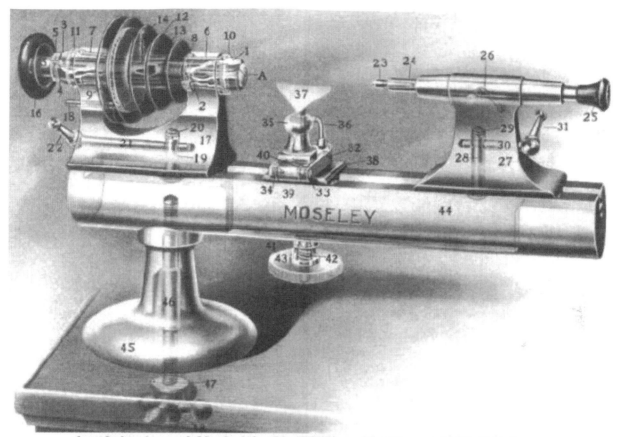

An early American-made Moseley lathe of the "WW" type with parts as annotated by the maker.

1. Headstock Spindle	2. Throat pin	3. Loose bearing	4. Loose bearing pin
5. Adjusting nut	6. Front bushing	7. Rear Bushing	8. Front inside shield
9. Rear inside shield	10. Front outside shield	11. Rear outside shield	
12. Pulley	13. Pulley Hub	14. Pulley screw	15. Draw-in spindle
16. Draw-in spindle wheel	17. Frame	18. Index pin	19. Bolt
20. Spring	21. Eccentric	22. Lever	23. Pointed Centre
24. Spindle	25. Spindle Button	26. Spindle Binder	27. Frame
28. Bolt	29. Spring	30. Eccentric	31. Lever
32. Slide	33. Pivot Screw	34. Pivot Screw	35. Post
36. Lever	37. T graver rest	38. Shoe	39. Shoe bolt

The work that can be performed by a lathe: tools.

Polishing pivots

Pegging

Re-pivoting [broken off pivots]

Straightening bent pivots

Making replacement clock and watch parts

Make your own bushings and taper pins

Repairing parts

Clock Marts

Organizations like the NAWCC hold annual marts where dozens of fellow members and clock hobbyists set out tables of clocks, practice movements, tools, books and materials for sale at reasonable prices. A swap meet dedicated to clock repair. These sellers hold a wealth of knowledge and can be a sauce of local mentors or support. There are often classes held at the same time. Contact the NAWCC to find a local upcoming mart.

Lessons Learned

From teaching my clock repair class, I can give some feedback that many students fail to learn the first time around. I will use this feedback to give you a heads up and an important recap on things to pay extra attention.

Many students seem to have a problem with the importance of pivot and pivot-hole polishing. It is important that whenever a movement is dismantled, the pivots and pivot holes be re-polished to a very high standard. Not just cleaned in soapy water, or even a good quality clock cleaning solution, not just making a dull pivot a little shinier. Not just removing grooves, but making the pivot very flat, smooth and glass shiny so you can see reflections in it.

Before putting the movement back together, test each wheel **individually** between the plates to make sure it spins very freely. Then test **two wheels** together and finally the complete train [without the 1st wheel or escapement], and make sure everything runs smoothly. I have countless times tried to help a student where the clock will not run when put back together. Invariably they have not followed this procedure and have to take the movement apart again to make small adjustments.

The escape wheel teeth must be in **perfect** condition for a clock to run. The slightest deviation to any tooth and the clock will stop or skip when the escapement gets to this tooth. I have yet to see a successful replacement of an escape wheel, even if the mating pallets are obtained with it.

Many students skip the step of making diagrams, especially noting the position of levers and pins. Or they lose the diagrams and or photos. It comes back to haunt them on assembly.

Clean all the parts as soon as you have dismantled the movement, but re-clean everything immediately before re-assembly and this time do not touch the parts you're your bare hands.

Always use the correct, well-fitting screwdriver for each screw. Take pride in keeping the screws in perfect condition.

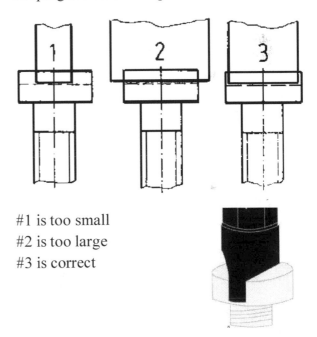

#1 is too small
#2 is too large
#3 is correct

Never, never, never open up a movement without completely letting down or capturing the mainspring, especially when adjusting the escapement or striking.

Clocks have only one known predator – the well-meaning clock repair person. Respect the clock, work slowly and methodically. Use the correct tools.

My Clock Won't Run

Conclusion

Caution, clock repairing is addictive.

This introduction is just the beginning of your learning curve. Before you know it, you will be buying old clocks that don't run and making them work. You will be able to repair clocks for family and friends or even to make extra money.

If you have been following along with a project clock, you have been performing engineering at the highest level, making repairs and adjustments to 1/1,000th of an inch.

Please bear in mind, the clock makers of the past served a five-year apprenticeship under the direction of a master clockmaker in order to learn and master the techniques, then another 5 years working for the master to fine-tune their skills. Then they could call themselves a Horologist. I feel privileged to work on these masterpieces. I urge you to work hard, enjoy the journey and have fun in your apprenticeship.

You are not alone. I strongly urge you to join a local clock club ie NAWCC or AWCI. Attend clock marts. Watch YouTube clock videos. Buy more books. Practice, Practice, Practice.

At the very least, monitor the free message boards at
www.mb.nawcc.org
www.awci.com/forum

There are many fine historical and modern timepieces in daily use and we need more people to service and maintain them.

WE NEED YOU!

Clock and Watch Associations

National Association of Watch and Clock Collectors (NAWCC)
717-684-8261
www.nawcc.org

American Watch-Clockmakers Institute (AWCI)
513-367-9800
www.awci.com

British Horological Institute (BHI)
(01636)813795
www.bhi.co.uk

Clock Supply Houses

TimeSavers (tools, parts, and supplies)
Box 12700
Scottsdale, AZ 85267
800-552-1520
480-483-3711
www.timesavers.com

S. LaRose Inc. (tools, parts, and supplies)
3223 Yanceyville St.
Greensboro, NC 27405
888-752-7673
336-621-1936
www.slarose.com

Norkro Clock Supplies (tools, parts, and supplies)
2209 NW Mill Pond Rd.
Portland, OR 97229
800-566-7576

www.norkro.com

Empire Clock (tools, parts, and supplies)
1295 Rice Street
St. Paul, MN 55117
800-333-8463
651-487-2885
www.empireclock.com

Merritts Antiques Inc. (tools, parts, and supplies)
1860 Weavertown Road
P.O. Box 277
Douglasville, PA 19518-0277
610-689-9541
www.merritts.com

Mile Hi Clock Supplies (Manufacturer of Keystone Tools and Mainspring Lubricants)
877-906-1200 Order Line
303-469-1220 Assistance
www.milehiclocksupplies.com

Butterworthsclocks (supplier of Hermle, Urgos, Kieninger Herr cuckoo etc. movements)
5300 59th. Ave. West
Muscatine, IA 52761
563-263-6759
www.buttersworthclocks.com

Meadows and Passmore [England]
www.m-p.co.uk

Horological Tools

Sherline Products Inc. (lathes, mills, and accessories)
3235 Executive Ridge
Vista, CA 92081-8527
800-541-0735
760-727-5857
www.sherline.com

P.P. Thornton LTD (clock wheel cutters)
The Old Bakehouse
Upper Tysoe
Warwickshire
CV35 0TR United Kingdom

TimeTrax (clock timing machines)
Can be purchased at www.merritts.com
Makers of TimeTrax
www.adamsbrown.com

MicroSet (clock timing machines)
805-687-5116 www.bmumford.com

Horological Book Sellers

Arlington Books
http://www.arlingtonbooks.com
US Books www.usbooks.com

Recommended Books
The Clock Repair First Reader.... P.E. Balcomb
The Clock Repair Primer.... P.E. Balcomb
The Top 300 Trade Secrets of a Master Clockmaker. J.M. Huckabee
Clock Repair Basics.... Steven Conover
Clock Repair Skills.... Steven Conover
Chime Clock Repair.... Steven Conover
Clock Repair Tips.... B.C. Tipton
Practical Clock Repairing.... Donald DeCarle
Clock Design & Construction

Frequently Asked Student Questions

I think I overwound the clock. It's wound all the way and the clock won't run.

In actual fact, it is almost impossible to overwind a clock. Once the coils of a flat mainspring are in firm contact with one another, the spring cannot be physically wound any tighter. The only way to truly overwind a clock spring is to turn it so tightly that the spring actually breaks. The most likely problem is that the lubrication on the mainspring has failed due to age.

As a lubricant ages, its viscosity slowly rises (it gets thicker). Eventually, a lubricant no longer acts as a lubricant and gets tacky. This causes the coils of the mainspring to physically stick together. In actual fact, it's time for a cleaning /overhaul to remove old lubricant and accumulated dirt and replace it with fresh lubricant specially designed for clocks.

My clock use to run a full week on a winding but now it will only run for a day or two.

The same answer as above. A clock that only runs a few days on a winding when it should run a week, likely has lubrication problems, although not usually the mainsprings. It is likely that the lubricant found in each bearing surface of the gears has failed and likely, there is a buildup of dirt and grime attracted by the lubricant. Time for a cleaning. Alternatively, the spring might have become "set" lost is elasticity. Time for a new spring.

My clock was just cleaned and it won't run for more than a few minutes even when fully wound. Also, I checked it with a level and it is level on the wall/mantle

My first suspicion when I hear this comment is to question whether the clock is in beat. A clock being in or out of beat has nothing to do with a clock being level. First, to explain what "in beat" means. A clock is in beat when ticks and tocks occur with the same time interval between each tick and tock. You can listen to a clock's ticking and make a pretty close approximation of an "in beat" condition.

If you have trouble hearing the difference between in and out of beat, purposely tilt the clock slightly left or right off level. It's easier to hear different time intervals when the out of beat condition is exaggerated. Sometimes, a clock can be knocked out of beat by over swinging the pendulum. Also, moving a clock from one location to another without immobilizing the pendulum can knock a clock out of beat. Some wall clocks have a degrees scale attached to the clock behind the tip of the pendulum. In such cases, I will set the clock up to be in beat when the tip of the pendulum is centered on this convenient scale.

My clock stops once an hour

Does the clock stop every time the hands are overlapping? If this is the case, then the most likely cause is that the hands are interfering with one another. It could also be a striking problem.

I was winding my clock and I heard a loud bang and now the clock won't wind.

In this case, the problem is usually related to one of two possible causes. Either the mainspring has broken, or, the ratchet pawl on the mainspring has failed. The ratchet mechanism is responsible for preventing the mainspring for unwinding as you wind a clock. It is the clicking that you hear as you wind. It is important to check out the rest of the mechanism after an explosive release of a mainspring as there is often other damage that occurs. Bent arbors and bent or missing teeth are the most common problems seen when a mainspring or ratchet fails.

I'm interested in going into the clock repair business. Where can I go to get training?

AWCI is the only establishment in the US which certifies professionals. They have home study courses, in-house training at their facility in Ohio, and professionals who travel around the country and do training. BHI, based in England, also certifies professionals and has a home study course as well as in-house training. Both institutes turn out some of the finest professionals in the business but their course studies are demanding.

The NAWCC's School of Horology is another resource for education. Although not able to professionally certify their students, it is a wonderful training ground for those interested. The school's disclaimer reads "The Avocational courses and the Specialty courses do not fall under the School's accreditation with ACCSCT. These courses are strictly taken as hobbyist courses or courses to further enhance the knowledge of people working in the industry." The NAWCC also has field suitcase courses which are organized through local NAWCC chapters around the country.

There are a number of books available if you are unable to afford to take classes and would like to be self-taught. The best books are DeCarle's "Clock Repair" and Goodrich's "The Modern Clock". These are available on-line from Arlington Books.

The only other way to learn the trade is to become an apprentice to a clockmaker. Ask around and see if there is anyone willing to train you but don't be disappointed if you don't find someone. Persons who are qualified to take on an apprentice, and have the time to do so, are few and far between.

How do I transport my clock?

If you're moving a clock that has a pendulum, please make sure you remove it from the clock and wrap it to keep it from damaging the movement or your case. If you cannot get the pendulum off by yourself, you can cushion and wrap it with towels or some other material to keep it from swinging wildly as you move it.

Why did my clock stop after running perfectly for so many years?

Clocks work great…until they stop. Over the years, the holes in the movement plates become worn and elongated, therefore misaligning the gears and wheels, causing the amount of force required to run the clock to be so great as to stop it. The oil dries up and becomes gummy, causing the clock to work dry and have excessive wear. Even with regular oiling, every clock will eventually wear out and stop working. Without regular oiling, they wear out even faster.

My clock is over 100 years old. Can you still get parts for it?

As you might guess, parts for antique clocks are not always available. Most clock repair shops do not have the expertise or equipment to fabricate or rebuild worn and damaged parts that were manufactured in the 18th or 19th centuries.

How do I reset my clock?

Since there are some older antique clocks whose hands cannot be turned backward, there is a common misconception that you must never turn the hands backward on any clock. It is okay to move the hands backward on all modern clocks and most antiques. If you try to move the hands backward and you feel resistance, don't force them. It is always okay to move the hands forward, waiting at each hour, ½ hour, or ¼ hour for the chimes & strikes.

Is my clock worth repairing?

I cannot answer this question specifically since each clock and clock owner is different, but I can share with you, what I feel is the best way to come to a decision.

There are two kinds of clocks we will consider here. The first type is a clock that has no emotional value to a person at all; it is simply a functioning clock that no longer works. In this case, the replacement value of the piece should factor into the decision. If the clock is going to cost as much or more to repair than it is to replace, you might as well replace it. An honest clockmaker will inform his customer when this is the case.

The other kind of clock is one that has either been passed down to its current owner through a family member, the current owner intends to pass it on to their children or the clock holds some special sentiment or meaning to the individual. In this case, the most important factor is not its replacement value, but its emotional or sentimental value. Because this type of clock is "one of a kind" and essentially irreplaceable, it is well worth whatever the cost of a proper repair would be.

Most of the time when dealing with a quality clock, even a complete overhaul of the clock movement is going to cost less than the clock's actual value. On some of the more common antique clocks, the cost will frequently come very close to or perhaps be a little more than its actual value and the more unusual or rare pieces will have a repair cost that will fall well below. Unless the clock has been purchased for "investment" reasons or for resale, the clock's emotional value should be considered first.

Should I replace my worn clock dial?

Many early American clocks had dials that were nothing more than a printed piece of paper glued to a metal dial pan. As these paper dials aged many of them have become extremely dirty and or worn badly.

Many times the customer will ask whether anything can be done about this and if it will affect the clock's value. The first thing I do is ask them if they are planning to sell the clock. If they are not, then the value of the clock after a dial replacement is really not a factor.

In the case of most common clocks, if the value of the clock is an important consideration in making the decision to replace or not, I will usually tell them that they have lost either way. If the clock's dial is in bad enough condition to consider a replacement then some of the clock's value is lost already. Whether the dirty, badly worn dial is left in place or the dial is replaced, when it comes time to sell the clock, the purchaser will likely want to pay less either way. If the purchaser is an investment style collector he will be less interested either way because he will only be looking for clocks in original and mint condition.

Therefore, unless the clock is rare or has great antique value I tell them they should do what they think will please them the most when they look up at their clock sitting on the shelf or hanging on the wall.

Should I refinish my clock case?

The answer to this question is essentially the same as the last one. However, I'll add this. Many people now watch the "Antique Roadshow" on TV. They have heard the appraiser's comments about how a particular item's value has been diminished due to refinishing. This certainly can be true. A very rare piece is often worth more even if the original finish is in very bad condition. Notice I said very rare! Most clocks that

people are bringing in for repair and considering the "refinish question" have clocks that are only worth several hundreds of dollars and although quite old are not rare at all. Frequently, the antique furniture in question on the "Antique Roadshow" is worth thousands and thousands of dollars, not a few hundred.

For most of my customers, the sentimental value far outweighs any antique value. Therefore they are repairing, refinishing and or replacing dials for their personal satisfaction, not for some future investment return.

Each clock owner must decide this question for themselves.

How often should my clock be oiled?

Manufacturers recommend oiling every 2 to 3 years, with a professional cleaning every 5 to 7 years. To get the most years out of your clock's movement, you should follow this advice.

Why does a clock have to be cleaned and oiled?

The movement or works of a clock is a mechanical device with gears moving in contact with other gears. These gears are made of steel. These steel axles (pivots) are positioned between two brass plates. The brass plates are usually coated with lacquer to prevent oxidation (tarnish). The holes in the brass where the steel axles rotate are NOT covered with lacquer. Tarnish will form in those areas unless protected by oil. This tarnish (oxide) breaks off in abrasive particles. It is like putting sand in a mechanical engine. These abrasive particles cause both the steel axles and the brass hole to wear out. The holes become egg shaped, and the gears no longer mesh properly, causing premature friction and wear. This is what kills a clock movement.

In addition, the fresh oil acts as a lubricant. The pendulum of a mechanical clock oscillates anywhere from 3,600 beats per hour to over 10,000 beats per hour. This goes on 24 hours a day, seven days a week for years. Can you imagine running your car or your sewing machine without oiling it? I have seen newer clocks be completely shot in 17 years without oiling. Older clocks will last longer due to thicker brass plates. At any rate, it appears that with proper oiling and cleaning the clock movement will last for 10 additional years or more.

Cuckoo Clock Questions

How do I set the time? It strikes 4 times on the half hour and once on the hour, and the time is not set right, and the hour hand is wrong.

Assume your clock is right and your hands are wrong. At least 90% of all cuckoo minute hands have a large round hole in them. If you get the hand off and it has a square hole in it just remove the hand and replace it in the next quarter or half hour. For the majority that does have the large round hole in them here is what you do. All the real adjustment takes place with the minute hand. Loosen the nut and remove the minute hand.

Stuck on the hand is a round piece of brass called a hand bushing. It has a square hole in it. This piece of brass needs to be turned one direction or the other and then just set the hand back on the clock. If it looks about right, put the nut on and tighten it and rotate the hand clockwise to see if it strikes the hour and half hour at the correct time. It probably won't be quite right the first time around. It rarely is for me. Be patient, adjust again.

Hold the minute hand still while you tighten the nut with a pair of pliers in the other hand. Once you get the minute hand striking where you want it to, then just move the hour hand to the last hours struck. The hour hand is a press on fit. Just turn it in either direction, then use your thumbnails to push down on each side of the hand near the shaft.

My clock runs for 3 or 4 minutes and then stops. What do I do?

First, make sure the clock is level on the wall. If it still doesn't run move the base slightly to the left and listen for an even tic-tic sound. Try running it again and if it still doesn't run move it slightly more to the left. If the tics don't even out and the clock still doesn't run then go back to level and repeat all the above by moving it to the right. Don't worry if the clock looks a little off level, right now we are trying to see if it will run. It may be off beat and still be able to run. You won't know unless you try this first.

My chain has come off the gear. What do I do?

First, we want to avoid the other chains coming off while you are fixing this one. Take a twist tie or a piece or string and capture the other chains together right at the base of the clock. Put the twist tie or string inside the links and tie it. If you put it around the chain they sometimes slip down the chain. This will keep those chains from coming off.

Now take the back off the clock and turn the clock upside down and give the loose chain a little slack. What you are trying to do is allowing enough slack to make a loop that you can hook around the gear sprocket.

It may take a few tries, but if you can see it there is a good chance you can do it. Use plenty of light. Some clocks have more room in them than others. If you succeed hold onto the chain while you upright the clock. Hang it on the wall and then remove the ties on the other chains.

My clock runs and keeps time, but the cuckoo bird won't come out?

Check and see if the shipping latch above the cuckoo door is open so the door will operate freely. If the clock is new or has been shipped back to you be sure you have removed the clips that hold the bellows together. Newer cuckoos may have a night shutoff feature. Some have a shut-off lever coming out of the side or a black heavy wire with a loop on it that comes out of the bottom of the clock. Move the lever down or pull the loop down and try the cuckooing again.

I've been told by others that my movement is worn out and needs replacing. Is that the only answer and how can I tell the difference?

Here is how to tell if your clock has significant wear that is causing it to stop running or cuckooing. Caution: do not lay the clock on its back or turn it over because the chains are only held on their sprockets by gravity and will come off. While looking in the back, pull up and down on one chain. In other words tug back and forth on the winding chain and the weight chain of one wheel.

Watch the back plate where the pivots come through the plate. Particularly the 2nd gear up from the bottom. If that steel pivot rod is jumping back and forth in the hole then you have significant wear.

Keep doing it and look at the other holes as you go up each train as you are pulling. If your case is big enough to get your hand in there just wiggle the bottom gear that the chain rides on. You will get the same effect.

Usually, the wear starts on that second gear but it is normal to have 2 or 3 gears worn that much on a clock that has been run a lot. The wear causes the gears to start separating and they don't mesh well. That causes it to lose power all the way up the train of gears. Try the time side also to check for wear. If one side is worn, it is likely that the other side isn't far behind.

How does the clock operate the music box?

Notice, this is for information only, pretty please don't try to fix this yourself or you will need me or someone else for sure. I always advise people to stay away from these and don't bend anything, but some are going to anyway and at least this gives them some idea of how they work. I'm going to try to tell you how the music box works. It may not be exactly what you have, but all are similar and will give your somewhere to start. There should be 2 connections from the movement to the music box. On some movements, both wires come from the same spot. On others, there is a flat strip of metal coming off the right-hand corner of the clock and a straight wire coming off the back center of the clock.

The flat strip of metal is hooked to a linkage that pulls a locking pin out of the music box at the top of the hour.

The music box tries to play but the fan is immediately stopped by the straight wire coming off the back of the clock. That wire will move back and forth as the clock cuckoos and when it finishes it is supposed to drop away just enough to let the fan rotate freely and the music will play and will lock itself back down. That is how it is supposed to work. Getting it to do that is extremely tricky. I sometimes spend as much as a whole day on adjusting one music box. Others may take me 10 minutes. There is only one sweet spot where everything will work.

Glossary of Clock Terms

A collection of meanings of common clock terms.

Alarm

Sound a clock makes to awaken the sleeper at a certain time. They come in various sounds: bell, double bell, chirp, beep, buzz, melody, etc.

Analog

The traditional look of time told by the angular positioning of hands on a dial.

Anniversary Clock

The name comes from the fact that when it was first invented, it needed winding just once a year on its anniversary (approximately 400 days). Characterized by a glass dome and a rotating pendulum. Also known as a "400 Day Clock".

Arabic Numerals

Most common number style (1, 2, 3, 4, etc.) used on clock dials.

Arch

The curved part of a clock case that resembles a door arch.

Beat

Term to describe the tick-tock of a mechanical timepiece. A clock is said to be in beat if the spacing between the tick and the tock are equal. If they are not equally spaced, the clock is out of beat and will generally stop after a short run.

Beveled Glass

Glass used in the clock case with an angled surface beginning about 3/4" from the edge.

Big Ben Gong

The deep-sounding chime that announces the hour. Modeled after the large bell clock in the tower of the House of Parliament in London.

Bim-Bam

Chime which only counts the hour and announces the half-hour.

Bob

Round, weighted end of a clock pendulum. Often made of brass.

Bow Top

A decorative feature found in certain mantel and wood case wall clocks. Characterized by a curved top section.

Bracket Clock

A term used by the British to indicate a table or shelf clock. Characterized by a square case with a handle on top, as it was designed to be carried from room to room.

Balloon Clock

Mantel or tabletop clocks shaped like hot-air balloons of the late 18th Century.

Burl

The decorative pattern in the wood grain caused by a series of irregularities that add to the character of the wood.

Cable Driven

Mechanical movement powered by weights hanging on cables wound with a key or crank.

Case/Cabinet

That which contains the clock, the housing or containment for the works (movement)

Carriage Clock

Small portable clock, usually has a brass case with glass sides and a decorative handle on top.

Center Shaft

The shaft that the minute hand is attached to, geared to make one revolution every 60 minutes.

Chain Driven

See also Weight Driven

Traditional cuckoo clock movement. It is driven by weights hung from chains with engaged sprockets.

Chapter Ring

A decorative ring on the clock dial upon which the hours are indicated. A feature of many traditional style mantel clocks. Also a prominent feature of clocks with skeleton movements.

Chime Melody

Tune played by the clock on the hour. A 4/4 Chime plays music and counts the hour, quarter hour, half hour, & three-quarter hour.

Chime Rods

Tuned rods which, when struck by small hammers powered by the clock movement, produce the chime melody and strike the hour. A component found in mechanical chime mantel and wall clocks.

Chip

Small silicon square onto which integrated circuits are imprinted. An integral part of the quartz movement.

Cornice

Topmost molding of a clock case. The 833-W is a great example of a well-defined cornice.

Crystal

A flat or convex piece of glass that covers the dial. Usually fitted into a brass bezel.

Day Ring

Divided ring on a lunar dial that indicates the days in the 29 1/2 day lunar cycle.

Dial

The face of a clock on which the hours are located.

Digital

Time display that uses no hands but shows the time in numbers and read out screen.

Drop Case

Wall clock with a lower case, which usually houses a swinging pendulum such as a Schoolhouse style clock.

Escapement

A means by which the pendulum allows the going train to operate at a regular interval, thus controlling the passage of time. It usually consists of anchor and escape wheel.

Etching

A process used to create a design in metal by the action of an acid. A feature found on the metal dials of many German Anniversary Clocks.

Finial

The spires, turnings, or decorative points on top of a clock case. Maybe wood or metal. Sometimes removable. Some are called "ball and spike", "urn", "acorn", etc.

Finish

Process and materials used to create an attractive wood surface. Examples include deep cherry, medium oak, mahogany, antique walnut, etc.

Grandfather Clock

The correct name is Long Case Clock [in Britain] or Tall Case Clock in the USA.

Hands

Used to mark hours, minutes, or seconds on a clock dial. Made of metal or plastic.

Inlay

Thin layers of wood applied to form a decorative pattern.

Keywound

A spring-driven clock that is wound with a key or crank.

Liquid Crystal Display (LCD)

Most frequently used in quartz alarms. Time is continuous, displayed in digital form.

Light Emitting Mode (LED)

Number telling the hours and minutes light up on a readout screen.

Lunar Dial

See also Moon Dial

An additional dial on a clock face that indicates the phase of the Moon each day.

Lyre

Ornamental feature on a pendulum resembling the ancient Greek instrument.

Marquetry

A type of decoration on wood made by inlaying wood veneers in elaborate designs.

Minute Track

Square or circular track divided into 60 equal segments. It may appear on the outer perimeter of the dial or in the dial center.

Moon Dial

See also Lunar Dial

An additional dial on a clock face that indicates the phase of the Moon each day.

Movement

Timekeeping mechanism of the clock, which also produces the strike and chime. Comes in quartz (battery), keywound, or weight-driven.

Pediment

The decorative top of a case, above the cornice.

Pendulum

A suspended, swinging rod and weight (bob) that regulates the clock movement in keywound/mechanical clocks. The pendulum in quartz (battery) clocks is purely decorative; the clock does not need it to properly function.

Pilaster

Decorative feature used to create the effect of columns on the clock cabinet.

Pinch-Waisted

Traditional clock style with the crown and case wider than the part of the clock enclosing the pendulum.

Quartz

Electronic transistorized movements that work on battery energy and require no winding or plug-in electricity. A tiny quartz crystal, vibrating at a high frequency, allows the clock mechanism to perform with extraordinary precision.

"R-A" Regulator

Slang term for wall regulator with "R-A" on the pendulum. "R" stands for retard by turning the adjusting nut toward R to lower the pendulum bob. "A" stands for advanced by turning the adjusting nut toward A to raise the pendulum bob.

Regulator

The mechanism that can be adjusted to make the clock more accurate. Sometimes the word "Regulator" is printed on the clock's glass, usually on Schoolhouse clocks.

Roman Dial

A dial with Roman numerals (I, II, III) frequently used in traditional style carriage, mantel, wall, tabletop, and anniversary clocks.

Rotating Pendulum

A feature found on both key-wound and quartz (battery) anniversary clocks. Characterized by decorative balls in crystal or metal finish.

Schoolhouse Clock

Traditional wood cabinet wall clock with a round or octagonal clock case and lower pendulum cabinet. Said to be true Early American Design. This style was most commonly found on classroom walls in American Colonial days.

St. Michael Chimes

Chimes originally installed in the St. Michael church steeple in Charleston, SC in 1764.

Scroll

A decorative ornament resembling a partially rolled scroll of paper.

Straight Sided

A style of clock cabinet in the same width from crown to base.

Strike

Chime or gong that indicates the hour.

Tambour

Style of clock case sometimes referred to as "Napoleon's Hat".

Tempus Fugit

Latin phrase meaning, "Time Flies". Sometimes engraved on a decorative panel on the clock dial or a plaque attached to the clock case.

Time train

The series of gears in the clock movement that operates the minute and hour hands (and second hand where applicable). The time-train is responsible for activating the chime in the movement.

Triple Chimes

Movement that plays 3 different chimes: Westminster, Whittington, St. Michael

Tubular Bell Chime

Long hollow tubes which, when struck by small hammers powered by the clock movement, produce the chime melody and strike the hour.

Verge

An escapement belonging to the Foliot and Verge. Not all escapements are verges.

Veneers

Thin layers of wood chosen for their attractive grain and permanently applied to a core material. The same material and method are used in making violin and guitar cases.

Weight Driven

See also Chain Driven

Traditional cuckoo clock movement. It is driven by weights hung from chains with engaged sprockets.

Westminster Chimes

Most popular tune used in chiming clocks. This famous tune originated in the Victorian clock towers in the House of Parliament in London.

Whittington Chimes

Chimes originally rang in the church of St. Mary Le Bow in London. Legend has it that a young boy running away from his master thought he heard them call out his name, telling him to turn back. Dick Whittington did and eventually became the Lord Mayor of London.

My suggested definition of time

The incremental measurement of the past, present and/or future.

9489199R00080

Printed in Germany
by Amazon Distribution
GmbH, Leipzig